1st EDITION

Perspectives on Diseases and Disorders

Food Allergies

Arthur Gillard

Book Editor

PERSPECTIVES
On Diseases & Disorders

GALE
CENGAGE Learning·

Detroit • New York • San Francisco • New Haven, Conn • Waterville, Maine • London

Elizabeth Des Chenes, *Director, Content Strategy*
Cynthia Sanner, *Publisher*
Douglas Dentino, *Manager, New Product*

For more information, contact:
Greenhaven Press
27500 Drake Rd.
Farmington Hills, MI 48331-3535
Or you can visit our Internet site at gale.cengage.com

For product information and technology assistance, contact us at

Gale Customer Support, 1-800-877-4253
For permission to use material from this text or product, submit all requests online at www.cengage.com/permissions

Further permissions questions can be e-mailed to permissionrequest@cengage.com

LIBRARY OF CONGRESS CATALOGING-IN-PUBLICATION DATA

Food allergies / Arthur Gillard, book editor.
    pages cm. -- (Perspectives on diseases and disorders)
  Includes bibliographical references and index.
  ISBN 978-0-7377-6354-6 (hardcover)
 1. Food allergy--Popular works. I. Gillard, Arthur.
  RC596.F638 2013
  616.97'3--dc23
                                        2013004165

Printed in the United States of America
1 2 3 4 5 6 7 17 16 15 14 13

CONTENTS

Foreword   7

Introduction   9

CHAPTER 1 Understanding Food Allergies

1. An Overview of Food Allergies   15
   Liz Swain

   Food allergies occur when the immune system
   mistakenly reacts to an otherwise benign food as if it
   were harmful, resulting in symptoms ranging from
   unpleasant (e.g., itching, diarrhea) to a severe and
   potentially fatal condition known as anaphylaxis.

2. Food Protein–Induced Enterocolitis
   Syndrome   26
   Allergies Sourcebook

   Food protein–induced enterocolitis syndrome is a
   rare but serious immune system reaction to food that
   shares some features with traditional food allergies
   but differs in significant respects.

3. Managing Food Allergies   33
   Cathy C. Ruff

   Food allergies are managed by identifying problem
   foods and eliminating them from the diet. Certain
   medications are also helpful for dealing with
   allergic symptoms, such as antihistamines and auto-
   injectable epinephrine.

4. Immunotherapy: An Experimental Treatment
   That May Help Alleviate Allergies   **39**

Elizabeth Landau

Immunotherapy is an experimental treatment in
which patients ingest gradually increasing amounts
of the foods they are allergic to in order to build up a
tolerance.

CHAPTER 2   Controversies About Food Allergies

1. Nut Allergy Is a Life-Threatening Condition
   That Needs to Be Taken Seriously   **45**

Robert A. Wood

Nut allergies are not an effect of mass hysteria but
are a serious and potentially fatal disease. Rigorous
precautions against potentially fatal anaphylaxis are
appropriate and necessary.

2. IgG Allergy Tests Are Not Effective   **50**

Helen Branswell

Popular immunoglobulin G (IgG) allergy tests,
often used by alternative health-care practitioners,
are completely ineffective at determining allergies,
according to allergy expert Elana Lavine.

3. IgG Allergy Testing Is an Effective
   Medical Practice   **55**

Jason Bachewich

IgG allergy testing is effective, and criticisms of it are
based on a misunderstanding of the nature of the
allergic process that the tests are measuring.

4. Genetic Engineering Can Produce
   Less-Allergenic Food Products   60

   Food, Nutrition & Science from the Lempert Report

   Genetic engineering can produce food with common
   allergens removed or reduced, which consumers will
   respond to positively.

5. Schools Need to Be Safe and Inclusive
   Places for Children with Food Allergies   65

   Kelly Rudnicki

   Schools need to do more to make conditions safe for
   children with food allergies, as well as to help them
   feel included in school activities.

6. Nothing to Sneeze at: Allergies May Be
   Good for You   71

   Melinda Wenner Moyer

   A controversial new theory states that allergies are
   a mechanism that evolved to protect people from
   harmful substances by either expelling them from the
   body or by motivating people to avoid the harmful
   substance.

CHAPTER 3   Personal Experiences with Food Allergies

1. An Allergy Doctor Describes Her
   Experience as the Mother of Three
   Food-Allergic Children   77

   Sarah M. Boudreau-Romano

   A pediatrician and allergist with several food-allergic
   children describes close calls her children have had
   and how this motivates her to find an effective food-
   allergy treatment.

2. Losing a Child to Food Allergies   **82**

Paul and Catrina Vonder Meulen

A father and mother describe the experience of losing their child to a fatal allergic reaction while on a shopping trip.

3. A Mother Puts Her Child's Food-Allergic Condition in Perspective   **88**

Kelley J.P. Lindberg

During a trip to the hospital to get an allergy blood test for her four-year-old food-allergic son, a mother is able to see his condition in a new light.

Glossary   **92**

Chronology   **96**

Organizations to Contact   **103**

For Further Reading   **108**

Index   **113**

FOREWORD

"Medicine, to produce health, has to examine disease."
—Plutarch

Independent research on a health issue is often the first step to complement discussions with a physician. But locating accurate, well-organized, understandable medical information can be a challenge. A simple Internet search on terms such as "cancer" or "diabetes," for example, returns an intimidating number of results. Sifting through the results can be daunting, particularly when some of the information is inconsistent or even contradictory. The Greenhaven Press series Perspectives on Diseases and Disorders offers a solution to the often overwhelming nature of researching diseases and disorders.

From the clinical to the personal, titles in the Perspectives on Diseases and Disorders series provide students and other researchers with authoritative, accessible information in unique anthologies that include basic information about the disease or disorder, controversial aspects of diagnosis and treatment, and first-person accounts of those impacted by the disease. The result is a well-rounded combination of primary and secondary sources that, together, provide the reader with a better understanding of the disease or disorder.

Each volume in Perspectives on Diseases and Disorders explores a particular disease or disorder in detail. Material for each volume is carefully selected from a wide range of sources, including encyclopedias, journals, newspapers, nonfiction books, speeches, government documents, pamphlets, organization newsletters, and position papers. Articles in the first chapter provide an authoritative, up-to-date overview that covers symptoms, causes and effects, treatments, cures, and medical advances. The second chapter presents a substantial number of opposing viewpoints on controversial treatments and other current debates relating to the volume topic. The third chapter offers a variety of personal perspectives on the disease or disorder. Patients, doctors, caregivers, and loved ones represent just some of the voices found in this narrative chapter.

Each Perspectives on Diseases and Disorders volume also includes:

- An **annotated table of contents** that provides a brief summary of each article in the volume.
- An **introduction** specific to the volume topic.
- Full-color **charts and graphs** to illustrate key points, concepts, and theories.
- Full-color **photos** that show aspects of the disease or disorder and enhance textual material.
- **"Fast Facts"** that highlight pertinent additional statistics and surprising points.
- A **glossary** providing users with definitions of important terms.
- A **chronology** of important dates relating to the disease or disorder.
- An annotated list of **organizations to contact** for students and other readers seeking additional information.
- A **bibliography** of additional books and periodicals for further research.
- A detailed **subject index** that allows readers to quickly find the information they need.

Whether a student researching a disorder, a patient recently diagnosed with a disease, or an individual who simply wants to learn more about a particular disease or disorder, a reader who turns to Perspectives on Diseases and Disorders will find a wealth of information in each volume that offers not only basic information, but also vigorous debate from multiple perspectives.

INTRODUCTION

Food allergies have been recognized since ancient times. The Hippocratic Corpus, written by a group of ancient Greek physicians, including Hippocrates of Kos (considered the father of medicine), about twenty-five hundred years ago, notes that foods safe for some people can harm others: "Cheese does not harm all men alike, some can eat their fill of it, while others come off badly."[1] In the first century, Roman philosopher and poet Lucretius observed that "what is food for some may be fierce poison for others."[2] Yet for much of human history, food allergies and related disorders did not seem to affect large numbers of people. The first sizable compendium of food-allergy cases was not published until 1969, and it speaks of the relative rarity of such cases up to that point.

But during the latter part of the twentieth century, the known incidence of allergies of all kinds increased dramatically. Scientists discovered in the late 1970s and early 1980s that a substantial increase had occurred in the number of reported asthma cases—an epidemic not just in the United States but around the world. Then in the 1990s it came to light that a second wave of increased allergies—this time food allergies—was taking place. In the United States Dr. Hugh Sampson reported that a twofold increase in allergic reactions to peanuts and other tree nuts occurred between 1985 and 1996. A doubling in the incidence of food allergies was described by doctors in England around the same time, and investigators in Germany, France, and Canada also reported significant increases of various food allergies in their respective populations. Many theories have been offered to explain the increase, but as of yet the cause or causes remains mysterious.

When someone has a food allergy, his or her immune system mistakenly identifies a nontoxic food as a dangerous foreign invader. When the food-allergic person is exposed to that food, the immune system response will cause symptoms ranging from uncomfortable to potentially fatal depending on factors such as the amount ingested, the exact nature of the particular allergy, and how severe the allergy is. Formerly innocuous food becomes a source of danger that can show up anywhere. As multiple-allergy sufferer Sandra Beasley wryly observes, "There's a reason they're called allergy 'attacks'; you never know where a food can be lurking."[3] Not surprisingly, this can have a negative impact on one's quality of life. As Sloane Miller, author of *Allergic Girl: Adventures in Living Well with Food Allergies,* notes,

> To avoid severe allergic reactions, millions of adults opt out of life's pleasures: kissing, dinner dates, social engagements, holidays and other celebrations, business lunches, and traveling to far-flung destinations—in other words, anywhere that food is involved, and that's pretty much everywhere. Even when they opt in, food-allergic adults are often actively fearful, anxious, or nervous. They can also feel ashamed, embarrassed, marginalized, isolated, lonely, and different because of their dietary restrictions. They often suffer in silence.[4]

Allergy expert Paul J. Hannaway agrees: "Patients and families with food allergy must enact significant lifestyle changes to prevent potentially life-threatening episodes of anaphylaxis and maintain health and safety. These changes are often a source of tremendous anxiety and stress for patients and their families."[5] According to Hannaway, studies of the emotional and psychological impact on those with allergies and their families show that children allergic to peanuts feel more threatened and restricted than those with diabetes, and children with peanut allergies and their families have greater stress and lifestyle im-

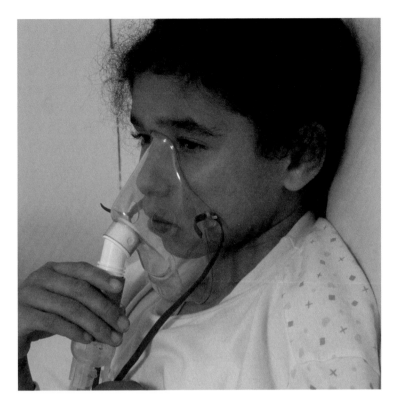

Asthma cases reached epidemic proportions in the late 1970s and early 1980s, followed in the 1990s by a marked increase in the number of reported allergy cases. (© **Bubbles Photolibrary/ Alamy**)

pairment than those suffering from rheumatoid arthritis or lupus erythematosus, both debilitating diseases.

In some cases, people who have experienced the most severe form of allergic reaction, anaphylactic shock, can be so traumatized by the experience that they develop the psychological condition known as post-traumatic stress disorder (PTSD). One allergy sufferer describes the experience:

> Up until four years ago, I was completely unaware I had any food allergies—until I had an anaphylactic attack. Some days I wake up and think the universe is playing a joke on me; some days I feel overwhelmed and have panic attacks from fear of eating anything that might cause an allergic reaction. My GP [general practitioner] calls it post-traumatic stress from the anaphylactic attack. All I know is that I'm scared all the time![6]

While it is important to recognize the very real dangers of food allergies, it is worth keeping in mind that the number of people who die from food-allergic reactions each year in the United States is relatively small, especially given the large number of people with food allergies. According to Nicholas Christakis, a medical sociology professor at Harvard University, fewer people die from food-allergic reactions each year than die as a result of bee stings.

After years of associating food with anxiety and danger, Miller realized that many of the traits that her experience with serious multiple food allergies instilled in her—such as obsessive attention to all the details of food preparation and ingredients, as well as her own experience of consuming food were also typical qualities of food lovers (or "foodies"), who share an obsession with food, albeit with a much more positive spin. With that insight, she found a way to turn her fear of food into a love of food:

> My relationship to food could have remained negative, traumatized, and distrustful, but instead it's transformed into something joyful, pleasurable, and gratifying.
>
> How did I reconcile those two disparate experiences? How does anyone? I was able to do it because I recognized that there's an inner foodie, or food lover, in me. I know there's one in every food-allergic person.
>
> Noted psychoanalyst Carl Jung is believed to have said, "The symptom is the symbolic solution." For those with adverse reactions to food, who, because of those reactions, end up hating food, the solution may be to embrace food, to love food. Think of it this way. Elie Wiesel, the noted author and humanitarian, is quoted as saying: "The opposite of love is not hate, it's indifference." In other words, if you hate what food can do to you, that means you also have the capacity to love what food can do for you.[7]

In many ways life is getting easier for food-allergy sufferers. There is greater awareness of the problem in the media and in the public in general than ever before. More restaurant owners and workers are knowledgeable about the issues and more accommodating to food-allergic patrons than in the past. Thanks to federal legislation, food labeling is improving. Specialty-food producers (and increasingly, mainstream ones) cater to the needs of those who must avoid certain ingredients. Software apps are now available to help people find restaurants and other resources that serve the needs of food-allergic people. And the scale of the problem, and the amount of attention devoted to it, has marshaled an increasing number of resources toward research into finding better ways to treat—and perhaps one day cure—food allergies.

In *Perspectives on Diseases and Disorders: Food Allergies* the contributing authors discuss and debate the causes of and controversies around this timely topic and some relate personal experiences of living with the condition.

Notes

1. Paul J. Hannaway, *On the Nature of Food Allergy: A Complete Handbook on Food Allergy for Patients, Parents, Restaurant Personnel, Child-Care Providers, Educators, School Nurses and All Health-Care Providers.* Marblehead, MA: Lighthouse, 2007, p. 2.
2. Hannaway, *On the Nature of Food Allergy,* p. 2.
3. Sandra Beasley, *Don't Kill the Birthday Girl: Tales from an Allergic Life.* New York: Crown, 2011, p. 4.
4. Sloane Miller, *Allergic Girl: Adventures in Living Well with Food Allergies.* Hoboken, NJ: Wiley, 2011, pp. 4–5.
5. Hannaway, *On the Nature of Food Allergy,* p. 4.
6. Miller, *Allergic Girl,* pp. 55–56.
7. Miller, *Allergic Girl,* p. 128.

CHAPTER 1

Understanding Food Allergies

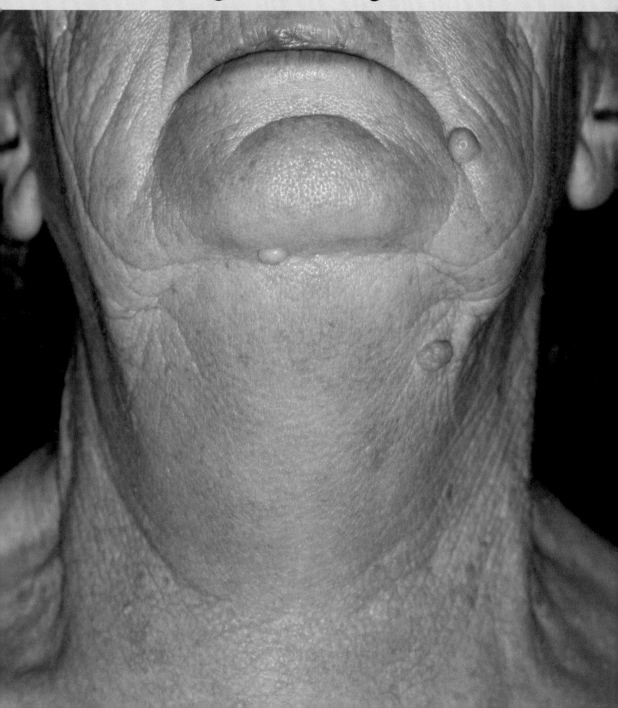

An Overview of Food Allergies

Liz Swain

Liz Swain is the author of several dozen encyclopedia articles in publications such as *The Gale Encyclopedia of Alternative Medicine* and *The Gale Encyclopedia of Nursing and Allied Health*. In the following selection, Swain describes food allergies as a health condition in which the immune system mistakenly reacts to an otherwise benign food as if it were harmful, resulting in symptoms ranging from unpleasant (e.g., itching, diarrhea) to a severe and potentially fatal condition known as anaphylaxis. She says food allergies, also known as food hypersensitivity, are often confused with food intolerance, a condition in which a person may react adversely to a food for reasons that do not involve the immune system; for example, they may react adversely to milk because they are unable to digest milk properly. According to the author, about 160 foods are known to induce allergic reactions, but 90 percent of allergic reactions result from just eight food families: eggs, milk, peanuts, tree nuts, soy, fish, shellfish, and wheat.

Photo on facing page. A woman with angioedema shows the swelling and rashes associated with an allergic reaction to certain foods.
(© Dr. P. Marazzi/Science Source)

SOURCE: Liz Swain, "Food Allergies," *The Gale Encyclopedia,* ed. Laurie J. Fundukian, 3 ed., 2011, pp. 1764– 1769, from Gale Encyclopedia of Medicine, 4E. © 2011 Cengage Learning.

Food allergies are the body's abnormal responses to harmless foods; the reactions are caused by the immune system's reaction to some food proteins.

Food Allergies and Food Intolerance

Food allergies are often confused with food intolerance. However, the two conditions have different causes and produce different symptoms. A food allergy is also known as food hypersensitivity. The allergy is caused when a person eats something that the immune system incorrectly identifies as harmful.

About 4% of adults have food allergies according to the National Institute of Allergy and Infectious Diseases (NIAID). The condition affects approximately 6 to 8% of children age 4 and younger.

The immune system works to protect the body and creates food-specific antibodies. The antibodies are proteins that battle antigens, substances that are foreign [to] or initially outside the body. The introduction of an antigen produces the immune response. Antibodies are created to destroy the antigen or counteract its effectiveness. . . .

The food that triggered that reaction is called an allergen. The antibodies are like an alarm system coded to detect the food regarded as harmful. The next time the person eats that food, the immune system discharges a large amount of histamine and [other] chemicals. This process, meant to protect the body against the allergen, causes an allergic reaction that can affect the respiratory tract, digestive tract, skin, and cardiovascular system.

Allergic reactions can occur in minutes or in up to two hours after the person eats the food. Symptoms include swelling of the tongue, diarrhea, and hives. In severe cases, the allergic reaction can be fatal. The most severe reaction is anaphylaxis, which can be life-threatening.

While food allergies involve the immune system, food intolerance is not related to the immune system. For ex-

According to the American Dietetic Association, most children with allergies today have reactions to eggs, milk, nuts, and soy. (© Igor Dutina/ Shutterstock.com)

ample, a person who is lactose intolerant has a shortage of lactase, the digestive enzyme that breaks down the sugar in milk and dairy products. That person could experience stomach pain or bloating several hours after drinking milk.

People who are food-intolerant can sometimes consume that food and not experience intolerance symptoms. Those diagnosed with food allergies must avoid the foods that produce the allergic reactions.

Food-Allergy Demographics

Although approximately 160 foods produce allergic reactions, about 90% of reactions are caused by some or all items within eight food families. These are milk, eggs, peanuts, tree nuts, fish, shellfish, wheat, and soy. These foods can cause severe reactions. The most adverse reactions are caused by peanuts and tree nuts. According to NIAID, about 0.6% of Americans are impacted by peanut allergies. Approximately 0.4% of Americans have allergic reactions to tree nuts.

Most children have allergies to eggs, milk, peanuts or tree nuts, and soy, according to the American Dietetic Association (ADA). The young generally outgrow their allergies. They are more likely to outgrow milk and soy allergies, according to NIAID. However, children and adults are usually allergic to peanuts and tree nuts for life. The most frequent causes of food allergies in adulthood are peanuts, tree nuts, fish, and shellfish.

Allergies are hereditary. There is a tendency for the immune system to create immunoglobulin E (IgE) antibodies in people with family histories of allergies and allergic conditions like hay fever and asthma, according to NIAID. The likelihood of a child having food allergies increases when both parents are allergic.

Furthermore, people are allergic to the foods that are eaten frequently in their countries. A rice allergy is more common in Japan, and codfish allergies occur more in Scandinavian countries, according to NIAID.

> **FAST FACT**
>
> Cases of food allergy increased by 18 percent between 1997 and 2007, according to a study by the Centers for Disease Control and Prevention published in 2008.

Causes and Symptoms

Food allergies are caused by the immune system's reaction to a food item that it deems harmful. When the food is digested, the immune system responds by creating immunoglobulin E antibodies as a defense. The antibodies are proteins found in the bloodstream. Formed to protect the body against harmful substances, the antibodies are created after the person's first exposure to the allergen.

The majority of food allergies are caused by foods in eight food families. In some of these families, *every* food causes an allergic reaction. In other families, such as shellfish, a person may be allergic to one species but able to eat others. The allergy-inducing foods include:

- *Milk.* The dairy family includes milk, ice cream, yogurt, butter, and some margarines. Nondairy foods that contain the milk protein casein must be avoided. Prepared foods that contain milk range from breads and doughnuts to sausage and soup, according to the ADA.

- *Eggs.* Although a person may be allergic to either the egg white or yolk, the entire egg must be avoided because there is a risk of cross-contamination. Eggs are an ingredient in mayonnaise. Moreover, products such as baked goods, breads, pasta, yogurt, and batter on fried foods may contain eggs. In addition, some egg-substitute products contain egg whites.

- *Peanuts.* Peanuts grow in the ground and are legumes like lentils and chickpeas. A person with a peanut allergy may not be allergic to other legumes or to tree nuts. Products to be avoided include peanuts, peanut butter, peanut oil, and some desserts and candy. In addition, some Asian dishes are prepared with a peanut sauce.

- *Tree nuts.* Tree nuts include almonds, cashews, pecans, walnuts, Brazil nuts, chestnuts, hazelnuts, macadamia nuts, pine nuts, pistachios, and hickory nuts. Products containing tree nuts include nut oil, desserts, candy, crackers, and barbecue sauce. A person may be allergic to one type of nut but able to eat others. That should be determined after consulting with a doctor.

- *Fish.* Fish allergy is generally diagnosed as an allergy to all fish species because the allergen is similar among the different species.

- *Shellfish.* Shellfish species include lobster, crab, crawfish, shrimp, clams, oysters, scallops, and other mollusks. An allergy to one type of shellfish may indicate an allergy to others.

- *Wheat.* Wheat is a grain found in numerous foods, including breads, cereals, pastas, lunch meats, and desserts. It is also found in products such as enriched flour and farina.

- *Soy.* The soybean is a legume, and people who have this allergy are rarely allergic to peanuts or other legumes. Soy is an ingredient in many processed foods, including crackers and baked goods, sauces, and soups. There is also soy in canned tuna, according to the ADA.

The Chemical Reaction

During the initial exposure to the allergen, many IgE antibodies are created. These attach to mast cells. These cells are located in tissues throughout the body, especially in areas such as the nose, throat, lungs, skin, and gastrointestinal tract. These are also the areas where allergic reactions occur.

The antibodies are in place, and a reaction is triggered the next time the person eats the food. As the allergen reacts with the IgE, the body releases histamine and other chemicals. Histamine is a chemical in the body's cells. When released during an allergic reaction, histamine and other chemicals cause symptoms like inflammation.

The type of allergic reaction depends on where the antibodies are released, according to NIAID. Chemicals released in the ears, nose, and throat could cause the mouth to itch. The person may also have difficulty breathing or swallowing. If the allergen triggers a reaction

Anaphylactic Reaction

When a food allergy develops, B cells—part of the body's immune system—develop immunoglobulin E (IgE) antibodies in response to food allergens that are mistakenly identified as harmful foreign invaders. The IgE antibodies attach to the surface of mast cells or basophils (white blood cells involved in defending the body from foreign invaders). When the food allergen is encountered again, it binds to the IgE antibodies that were previously created, causing the cells to degranulate, meaning they release chemicals, such as histamine, stored in granules inside the cell. Those chemicals in turn cause various phenomena involved in an allergic or anaphylactic reaction. For example, histamine causes tiny blood vessels (capillaries) to expand and become more permeable, which causes tissue swelling.

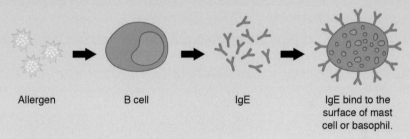

| Allergen | B cell | IgE | IgE bind to the surface of mast cell or basophil. |

Allergen triggers production of IgE antibodies.

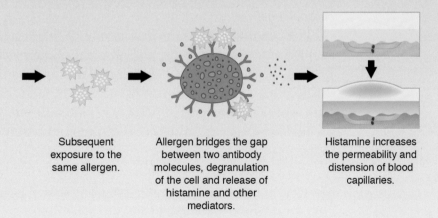

| Subsequent exposure to the same allergen. | Allergen bridges the gap between two antibody molecules, degranulation of the cell and release of histamine and other mediators. | Histamine increases the permeability and distension of blood capillaries. |

in the gastrointestinal tract, the person could experience stomach pain or diarrhea. An allergic reaction that affects skin cells could produce hives. This condition, also known as urticaria, is an allergic reaction characterized by itching, swelling, and the presence of patchy red areas called weals.

Severe Allergic Reaction

Anaphylaxis is a severe allergic reaction that is potentially life-threatening. Also known as an anaphylactic reaction, this condition requires immediate medical attention. The reaction occurs within seconds or up to several hours after the person has eaten the allergy-inducing food.

Symptoms can include difficulty breathing, a tingling feeling in the mouth, and a swelling in the tongue and throat. The person may experience hives, vomiting, abdominal cramps, and diarrhea. There is also a sudden drop in blood pressure. Anaphylaxis may be fatal if not treated promptly.

Each year, some 150 Americans die from food-induced anaphylaxis, according to NIAID. The casualties are generally adolescents and young adults. The risk increases for people who have allergies and asthma. Also at increased risk are people who have experienced previous episodes of anaphylaxis.

The peanut is one of the primary foods that trigger an anaphylactic reaction. Tree nuts also cause the reaction. The nuts generally linked to anaphylaxis are almonds, Brazil nuts, cashews, chestnuts, hazelnuts, macadamia nuts, pecans, pine nuts, pistachios, and walnuts. Fish, shellfish, and eggs can also set off the reaction, according to the ADA.

Cross-reactivity is the tendency of a person with one allergy to react to another allergen. A person allergic to crab might also be allergic to shrimp. In addition, someone with ragweed sensitivity could experience sensations when trying to eat melons during ragweed pollinating season, according to NIAID. The person's mouth would start itching, and the person would not be able to eat the melon. The cross-reaction happens frequently with cantaloupes. The condition is known as oral allergy syndrome. . . .

Allergen Avoidance and Food Labels

The treatment for food allergies is to avoid eating the food that causes the allergy. This preventive treatment includes reading food labels. Manufacturers are required by the U.S. Food and Drug Administration to list a product's ingredients on the label. However, if there is a question about an ingredient, the person should contact the manufacturer before eating the food. When dining out, people should ask whether food contains the allergen.

When reading food labels, people with food allergies should know that:

- Words indicating the presence of milk include lactose, ghee, and whey.
- Words signifying eggs in a product include albumin, globulin, and ovomucin.
- While it is apparent that peanuts are an ingredient in a product like peanut butter, there could be peanuts in hydrolyzed plant protein and hydrolyzed vegetable protein.
- People with tree nut allergies should carefully read the labels of products such as cereals and barbecue sauces.
- The American Dietetic Association cautions that surimi, an imitation seafood, is made from fish muscle. Furthermore, fish such as anchovies are sometimes an ingredient in Worcestershire sauce.
- Words on labels that signal the presence of wheat include gluten, seitan, and vital gluten.

Parents of children with food allergies need to monitor their children's food choices. They also must know how to care for the child if there is an allergic reaction. Parents need to notify the child's school about the condition. Caregivers should be informed, too. Both the school and caregivers should know how to handle an allergic reaction. Care must be taken because a highly allergic person could react to a piece of food as small as 1/44,000 of a peanut kernel, according to NIAID. . . .

Living with Severe Allergies

Despite precautions, people may accidentally eat something that causes an allergic reaction. People with severe allergies must be prepared to treat the condition and prevent an anaphylactic reaction. A medical alert bracelet should be worn. This informs people that the person has a food allergy and could have severe reactions.

To reduce the risks from an anaphylactic reaction, the person carries a syringe filled with epinephrine, also known as adrenaline. This is a prescription medication sold commercially as the EpiPen auto-injector. While prices vary, a syringe costs about $50.

The person with allergies must know how to inject the epinephrine. It is helpful for other family members to know how to do this, and parents of an allergic child must be trained in the procedure.

The person is injected at the first sign of a severe reaction. Medical attention is required, and the person should be taken to an emergency room. The person will be treated and monitored because there could be a second severe reaction about four hours after the initial one. . . .

Prognosis and Prevention

Food allergies cannot be cured, but they can be managed. The allergen-inducing foods should be avoided. These foods should be replaced with others that provide the vitamins and nutrients needed for a healthy diet. . . .

People prevent the return of food allergies by following treatment guidelines. These include avoiding the foods that cause allergic reactions, reading food labels, and taking measures to prevent an anaphylactic reaction.

Anaphylaxis is a major concern after a diagnosis of severe food allergies. To reduce the risks associated with this reaction, people with food allergies should wear medical alert bracelets and never go anywhere without epinephrine. If possible, family members or friends of adults with allergies should learn how to administer this medication.

The American Dietetic Association advises people to develop an emergency plan. ADA recommendations include preparing a list of the foods the person is allergic to, three emergency contacts, the doctor's name, and a description of how to treat the reaction. This list is kept with the epinephrine syringe.

Food Protein–Induced Enterocolitis Syndrome (FPIES)

Allergies Sourcebook

The following selection is taken from the *Allergies Sourcebook*, published by Omnigraphics, Inc. Food protein–induced enterocolitis syndrome (FPIES) is an unusual type of food allergy that affects the gastrointestinal (GI) tract. Whereas the vast majority of food allergies are immune system responses mediated by immunoglobulin-E (IgE) antibodies, FPIES is believed to be cell-mediated, a different type of immune system reaction. As a result, FPIES manifests differently than typical food allergies. Whereas typical allergies involve an immediate reaction, FPIES reactions generally take place hours after the offending food has been ingested and involve symptoms such as vomiting and diarrhea. Typical allergy symptoms such as swelling and hives do not occur with FPIES, and standard allergy tests do not detect this disorder. Most children with FPIES outgrow the condition by age three, but that may not be the case with all patients. FPIES can coexist with other allergies or food intolerances.

FPIES is food protein–induced enterocolitis syndrome. It is commonly pronounced "F-Pies," as in "apple pies," though some physicians may refer to it as FIES (pronounced "fees," considering *food-protein* as one word). Enterocolitis is inflammation involving both the small intestine and the colon (large intestine).

FPIES is a non-IgE [immunoglobulin E]–mediated immune reaction in the gastrointestinal system to one or more specific foods, commonly characterized by profuse vomiting and diarrhea. FPIES is presumed to be cell mediated. Poor growth may occur with continual ingestion. Upon removing the problem food(s), all FPIES symptoms subside. (Note: Having FPIES does not preclude one from having other allergies/intolerances to the food.) The most common FPIES triggers are cow's milk (dairy) and soy. However, any food can cause an FPIES reaction, even those not commonly considered allergens, such as rice, oats, and barley.

A child with FPIES may experience what appears to be a severe stomach bug, but the "bug" only starts a couple of hours after the offending food is given. Many FPIES parents have rushed their children to the ER [emergency room], limp from extreme, repeated projectile vomiting, only to be told, "It's the stomach flu." However, the next time they feed their children the same food, the dramatic symptoms return.

IgE-Mediated and Cell-Mediated Reactions

IgE stands for immunoglobulin E. It is a type of antibody, formed to protect the body from infection, that functions in allergic reactions. IgE-mediated reactions are considered immediate hypersensitivity immune system reactions, while cell-mediated reactions are considered delayed hypersensitivity. Antibodies are not involved in cell-mediated reactions. For the purpose of understanding FPIES, you can disregard all you know about IgE-mediated reactions.

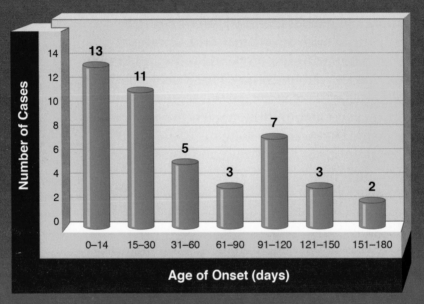

Age Distribution for the Onset of Food Protein–Induced Enterocolitis Syndrome (FPIES)

In a study of forty-four patients with food protein–induced enterocolitis syndrome (FPIES), more than half of the patients developed symptoms within thirty days after birth. All of the patients with FPIES were having symptoms by 180 days after birth.

Number of Cases

14
12
10
8
6
4
2
0

13
11
5
3
7
3
2

0–14   15–30   31–60   61–90   91–120   121–150   151–180

Age of Onset (days)

Taken from: Yitzhak Katz et al. "The Prevalence and Natural Course of Food Protein–Induced Enterocolitis Syndrome to Cow's Milk: A Large-Scale, Prospective Population–Based Study." *Journal of Allergy and Clinical Immunology*, vol. 127, no. 3, March 2011, pp. 647–653. www.sciencedirect.com/science/article/pii/S0091674911000108.

FPIES reactions often show up in the first weeks or months of life, or at an older age for the exclusively breast-fed child. Reactions usually occur upon introducing the first solid foods, such as infant cereals or formulas, which are typically made with dairy or soy. (Infant formulas are considered solids for FPIES purposes.) While a child may have allergies and intolerances to food proteins they are exposed to through breast milk, FPIES reactions usually do not occur from breast milk, regardless of the mother's diet. An FPIES reaction typically takes place when the child has directly ingested the trigger food(s).

As with all things, each child is different, and the range, severity, and duration of symptoms may vary from reaction to reaction. Unlike traditional IgE-mediated allergies, FPIES reactions do not manifest with itching, hives, swelling, coughing, or wheezing, etc. Symptoms typically only involve the gastrointestinal system, and other body organs are not involved. FPIES reactions almost always begin with delayed onset vomiting (usually 2 hours after ingestion, sometimes as late as 8 hours after). Symptoms can range from mild (an increase in reflux and several days of runny stools) to life threatening (shock). In severe cases, after repeatedly vomiting, children often begin vomiting bile. Commonly, diarrhea follows and can last up to several days. In the worst reactions (about 20% of the time), the child has such severe vomiting and diarrhea that s/he rapidly becomes seriously dehydrated and may go into shock.

Shock is a life-threatening condition. Shock may develop as the result of sudden illness, injury, or bleeding. When the body cannot get enough blood to the vital organs, it goes into shock.

Signs of shock include:

- weakness, dizziness, and fainting;
- cool, pale, clammy skin;
- weak, fast pulse;
- shallow, fast breathing;
- low blood pressure;
- extreme thirst, nausea, or vomiting;
- confusion or anxiety

FPIES Treatment

Always follow your doctor's emergency plan pertaining to your specific situation. Rapid dehydration and shock

> **FAST FACT**
>
> A 2009 study found that vomiting was the most common symptom in FPIES patients, occurring in 100 percent of cases; 85 percent also experienced lethargy, 67 percent pallor, and 24 percent diarrhea.

are medical emergencies. If your child is experiencing symptoms of FPIES or shock, immediately contact your local emergency services (911). If you are uncertain if your child is in need of emergency services, contact 911 or your physician for guidance.

The most critical treatment during an FPIES reaction is intravenous (IV) fluids, because of the risk and prevalence of dehydration. Children experiencing more severe symptoms may also need steroids and in-hospital monitoring. Mild reactions may be able to be treated at home with oral electrolyte rehydration (e.g., Pedialyte®). . . .

FPIES does not usually require epinephrine . . . because epinephrine reverses IgE-mediated symptoms, and FPIES is not IgE-mediated. Based on the patient's history, some doctors might prescribe epinephrine to reverse specific symptoms of shock (e.g., low blood pressure). However, this is only prescribed in specific cases.

The most common FPIES triggers are traditional first foods, such as dairy and soy. Other common triggers are rice, oats, barley, green beans, peas, sweet potatoes, squash, chicken, and turkey. A reaction to one common food does not mean that all of the common foods will be an issue, but patients are often advised to proceed with caution with those foods. Note that while the above foods are the most prevalent, they are not the exclusive triggers. Any food has the potential to trigger an FPIES reaction. Even trace amounts can cause a reaction.

FPIES is difficult to diagnose, unless the reaction has happened more than once, as it is diagnosed by symptom presentation. Typically, foods that trigger FPIES reactions score a negative with standard skin and blood allergy tests . . . because those tests look for IgE-mediated responses. However, as stated before, FPIES is not IgE-mediated.

Atopy patch testing (APT) is being studied for its effectiveness in diagnosing FPIES, as well as predicting whether the problem food is no longer a trigger. Thus,

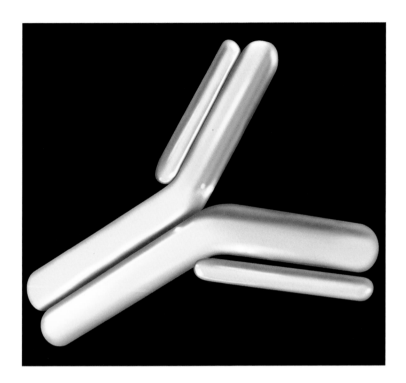

A representation of the antibody immunoglobulin E (IgE), which is formed to protect the body from infection. (© **UIG via Getty Images**)

the outcome of APT may determine whether the child is a potential candidate for an oral food challenge (OFC). APT involves placing the trigger food in a metal cap, which is left on the skin for 48 hours. The skin is then watched for symptoms in the following days after removal. . . .

Outgrowing FPIES

Treatment varies, depending on the patient and his/her specific reactions. Often, infants who have reacted to both dairy and soy formulas will be placed on hypoallergenic or elemental formulas. Some children do well breast-feeding. Other children who have fewer triggers may just strictly avoid the offending food(s).

New foods are usually introduced very slowly, one food at a time, for an extended period of time per food. Some doctors recommend trialing a single food for up to 3 weeks before introducing another.

Because it's a rare, but serious, condition, in the event of an emergency, it is vital to get the correct treatment. Some doctors provide their patients with a letter containing a brief description of FPIES and its proper treatment. In the event of a reaction, this letter can be taken to the emergency room with the child. . . .

Many children outgrow FPIES by about age 3. Note, however, that the time varies per individual and the offending food, so statistics are a guide, not an absolute. In one study, 100% of children with FPIES reactions to barley had outgrown and were tolerating barley by age 3. However, only 40% of those with FPIES to rice, and 60% to dairy tolerated it by the same age.

Managing Food Allergies

Cathy C. Ruff

Cathy C. Ruff is an associate professor in the Child Health Associate/ Physician's Assistant Program, Department of Pediatrics, University of Colorado at Anschutz Medical Center in Aurora. In the following viewpoint she focuses on management of food allergies in children, although her guidelines are applicable to teenage and adult patients as well. According to Ruff, avoidance of allergy-causing foods, nutritional counseling, and education are needed for healthy living with food allergies. She says that dietary avoidance should occur only in cases of documented food allergies. Education and nutritional counseling is needed to teach the patient or caregivers how to avoid dangerous foods—for example, by reading food labels properly. Ruff also describes medications that are helpful in managing food allergies. Antihistamines are useful for mild allergic reactions, and epinephrine is needed in cases of severe allergic reactions. If the allergy affects breathing, a bronchodilator (which increases air flow in the lungs) is recommended.

Food allergy in children [or adults] can be managed with dietary avoidance, nutritional counseling and education for the patient and family. Dietary avoidance is recommended for [those] with *documented* IgE [immunoglobulin E]—or non-IgE—mediated food allergy (i.e., positive results on the history, physical examination, laboratory findings, and oral food challenge). Dietary avoidance is not recommended for [those] without documented allergy. . . .

While there are different types of avoidance or elimination diets, the basic concept is to remove the suspected food for two to eight weeks. Symptoms will resolve if they are food-related and remain if they are not food-related. The diet must be monitored for nutritional adequacy; duration depends on the disease as well as on how well the patient's nutritional needs are being met.

Elimination Diets and Nutritional Counseling

Limited elimination diets are typically employed when the [health-care] provider suspects one of the more commonly allergenic foods (cow's milk, egg, wheat, soy, fish). . . .

Oligoantigenic elimination diets are useful when allergy to a large number of foods is suspected. This diet includes only those foods that have a low likelihood of allergenicity. The elemental diet, which can be most useful for infants, consists of a hypoallergenic (amino acid–based) formula with a few "safe" foods added, depending on the patient's age. This is useful when allergy to a large number of foods is suspected or for infants who are not yet eating solid food. Compliance is an issue after infancy because children outside early infancy are less likely to transition easily to a hypoallergenic formula, and older children and their parents will have difficulty with a diet that includes very few foods.

Nutritional counseling consists of instruction on which specific foods to avoid and on proper reading of food labels and information on avoidance of those foods labeled as "this product may contain trace elements" of the identified allergen. The reason for avoiding such foods is that there is no way to know how much allergen might be present in the packaged food. There may be none, or there may be a large amount. This means the patient may be able to eat the food on one occasion,

Nutritional counseling includes instruction on specific foods to avoid and the proper reading of food labels to avoid allergens.
(© Tim Gainey/Alamy)

feel safe in eating it again, and then get a package with a much larger volume of allergen the next time. The potential for severe reaction may then be more likely.

Children [or adults] with multiple food allergies should be referred to a dietitian or nutritionist to ensure that their dietary needs are being met. . . .

Because food allergy carries a risk of severe reaction and, potentially, death, patients and their families must have psychological support. Connecting families with support groups, counseling, or others with similar concerns is vital.

Medications for a Range of Sensitivity

While no preventive measures are currently recommended, patients with food allergy must be prescribed epinephrine, typically in the form of an auto-injectable unit for ease of use. Epinephrine is indicated in the treatment of acute, systemic allergic reactions [anaphylactic shock].

Antihistamines are used for managing nonsevere allergic reactions. Bronchodilators should be used if respiratory symptoms occur with exposure to the suspected food. Allergen-specific oral and sublingual immunotherapy is currently under study for inducing clinical desensitization [i.e., reducing reactivity to allergens] but is not recommended for use in clinical practice.

Patients should be instructed to use an antihistamine if physical contact with an allergenic food causes cutaneous [skin], ocular [eye or vision], or upper-respiratory-tract symptoms. Diphenhydramine [Benadryl] is the antihistamine of choice and should be administered in liquid or chewable form for most rapid effect. . . .

Auto-injectable epinephrine must be administered promptly after the ingestion of an allergenic food. This is first-line treatment in all cases of suspected anaphylaxis.

FAST FACT

The Food Allergen Labeling and Consumer Protection Act (FALCPA) requires all commercial food labels to clearly indicate the presence of any of the eight major food allergen families.

Causes of Accidental Food-Allergen Ingestion in Small Children

During a three-year study of five hundred food-allergic infants and young children, 72 percent of the subjects had allergic reactions. In 87 percent of the cases the reaction was due to accidental exposure. The pie chart below shows the circumstances behind the accidental exposures.

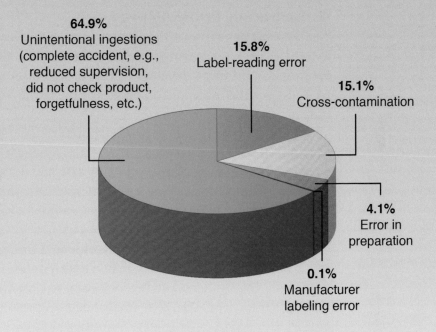

64.9%
Unintentional ingestions (complete accident, e.g., reduced supervision, did not check product, forgetfulness, etc.)

15.8%
Label-reading error

15.1%
Cross-contamination

4.1%
Error in preparation

0.1%
Manufacturer labeling error

Taken from: David M. Fleischer et al. "Allergic Reactions to Foods in Preschool-Aged Children in a Prospective Observational Food Allergy Study." *Pediatrics*, published online June 25, 2012. http://pediatrics.aapublications.org/content/early/2012/06/20/peds.2011–1762.full.pdf+html.

Delayed or improper use of the auto-injectable unit is a major cause of death.

Beyond inappropriate use of epinephrine, individuals who are at highest risk of death are adolescents and young adults, people with known food allergy and previous history of anaphylaxis, people with asthma (especially if poorly controlled), and people with peanut or tree-nut allergies.

In addition to these medication recommendations, providers should suggest that patients wear a medical alert bracelet and provide them with an appropriate action plan. An example of such a plan is available from the Food Allergy and Anaphylaxis Network. The purpose of the action plan is to outline the early signs and symptoms of a reaction, when it is appropriate to use antihistamines, when to use epinephrine and when to call 911.

Outgrowing Food Allergy

Tolerance is defined as either having naturally outgrown a food allergy or having received therapy so clinical symptoms no longer develop following ingestion of the food. In general, symptoms and exposure (accidental or not) are monitored over time. . . .

Many specialists will perform annual serum testing in children who have cow's milk, egg, soy or wheat allergies because these are commonly outgrown by the age of 5 years. Testing for peanut, tree-nut, fish, and shellfish allergies may be performed every two to three years, as these allergies are typically not outgrown. . . .

The reason tor retesting is to acquire data on specific IgE levels. With food allergies that are more commonly outgrown, the clinician will see a gradual decline in specific IgE levels over time. One may consider repeating an oral food challenge [deliberate exposure to a suspected allergy-triggering food under medical supervision] based on the lowered levels.

Rechallenge also might be considered when a child enters kindergarten. If the child has not already outgrown the allergy, parents may wish to know whether the youth will react if exposed to the food in question. In addition, the parent will have less control over what the child eats once he or she reaches school age, so a clearer understanding of what might happen upon exposure is key for both the child and the family. When considering whether or not to rechallenge a child, consultation with a provider who specializes in the treatment and management of food allergy is recommended.

Immunotherapy: An Experimental Treatment That May Help Alleviate Allergies

Elizabeth Landau

Elizabeth Landau is a health writer and blogger for CNN Health. In the following viewpoint she describes a study by researchers at the University of North Carolina on a promising new therapy for food-allergy sufferers called immunotherapy. In this experimental treatment, children with food allergies are given gradually increasing amounts of the food they are allergic to—starting with a minuscule dose—so that they can build up a tolerance to the food. By twenty-two months of egg immunotherapy, three-quarters of the children in the study were able to eat eggs safely. According to the author, this is a preliminary study and more research is needed. She cautions that this would be very dangerous to try without medical supervision.

With food allergies still on the rise and no clear answer about their causes, parents of allergic children anxiously await the development of an effective treatment to prevent life-threatening reactions.

SOURCE: Elizabeth Landau, "Food Allergy Treatment Shows Promise," *CNN*, July 18, 2012. Copyright © 2012 by CNN. All rights reserved. Reproduced by permission.

Researchers are making progress with a method for helping children with food allergies develop a tolerance for foods they otherwise couldn't eat. The technique is called immunotherapy. The basic idea is to give an allergic child extremely small quantities of the allergen and increase the dosage over time.

A [July 2012] study, published in the *New England Journal of Medicine*, is particularly exciting because it followed children with an egg allergy for one year after they stopped receiving immunotherapy treatment and found some success in that group. But more than half of the children did not show this immunity and doctors still don't know why.

Hope for the Future

"It really does give us great hope that there can be a treatment developed in the future," said Dr. Wesley Burks, chairman of the department of pediatrics at UNC [University of North Carolina] School of Medicine and chief physician at North Carolina Children's Hospital.

About 4% to 6% of children in the United States have food allergies, according to the Centers for Disease Control and Prevention. Some will outgrow their allergies, but others—especially children who are allergic to peanuts, tree nuts, fish and shellfish—will likely have to avoid certain foods for life. If they don't, they risk reactions ranging from mild itching and hives to airway blockages and even death. . . .

The immunotherapy approach has already been tried with peanuts and milk in small trials.

In this new study, researchers examined 55 children between ages 5 and 11 who were allergic to eggs. Forty of them received immunotherapy (controlled doses of egg white powder) and 15 of them received a placebo treatment.

By 22 months of treatment, 75% of kids who got the immunotherapy were considered "desensitized" to eggs.

Researchers found that 10 kids who had undergone the immunotherapy were eating eggs on their own a year

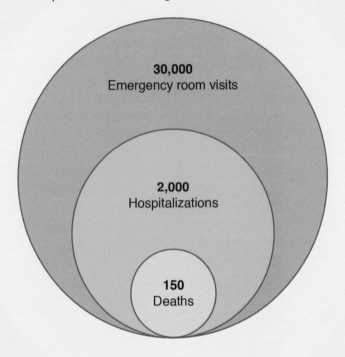

The Annual Toll of Food-Related Anaphylaxis in the United States

Food allergies have serious health consequences. Experimental treatments such as immunotherapy have the potential to significantly reduce the impact of serious allergic reaction.

30,000
Emergency room visits

2,000
Hospitalizations

150
Deaths

Taken from: "Food Allergies: What You Need to Know." US Food and Drug Administration, May 14, 2012. www.fda.gov/food/resourcesforyou/consumers/ucm079311.htm.

after the treatment ended, without symptoms. This was out of an initial group of 30 who took the treatment and could pass a food challenge (eating egg without incident) after 22 months of therapy.

Weighing the Risks

It's important to note, however, that about 15% of kids receiving the immunotherapy treatment dropped out of the trial—mostly because of allergic reactions, according to the study. Before this method could become the standard of care, doctors must further investigate what are the risks of undergoing treatment compared with just trying to live with the allergy and avoiding the offending food, the authors wrote. And the study authors can't totally rule out the possibility that some children were in the process of naturally outgrowing their egg allergies.

This is the largest blind, multisite trial of this kind, and the first to look at what happens after the treatment is over for such a significant period of time, Burks said.

A study in the *New England Journal of Medicine* that followed children with an egg allergy for one year after they received immunotherapy found the treatment to be successful in only about half the children. Doctors do not know why the other half of the group did not develop immunity. (© Lea Paterson/Alamy)

Ruslan Medzhitov, professor of immuno-biology at Yale School of Medicine, called this study a "very important investment" because it's moving toward a treatment. He believes it could become a standard of care if researchers figure out why some children respond perfectly to immunotherapy and others don't, and whether the outcome is truly a long-term immune tolerance of allergens.

It'll be another five to 10 years before this kind of thing could be widely available, Burks says.

In the meantime, don't try this at home. This procedure was done in a medical setting under tightly controlled conditions; parents should not attempt to inoculate their own allergic children against potentially deadly foods.

> **FAST FACT**
>
> A 2011 study published in the *Journal of Allergy and Clinical Immunology* suggests that consuming baked forms of milk and egg allergens might help some children develop tolerance to those foods.

Reducing the Risk of Hidden Allergens

Eggs can be hidden in all sorts of food products, which is why parents of children with this allergy need to be extremely cautious because even a single bite of a cooked egg can trigger a severe allergic reaction in some children.

"It's a huge strain on a family's quality of life because there's always this worry, no matter where you are or what you're doing: I hope my child is safe," says Dr. Ruchi Gupta, assistant professor of pediatrics and health services researcher at Northwestern University and Children's Memorial Hospital. . . .

Gupta's 6-year-old daughter is allergic to tree nuts and peanuts. There's always a fear that she might accidentally ingest a problematic food when she's at camp or school, Gupta said.

"Having something like immunotherapy, where I feel like she could start on small doses and gradually work her way up, would be amazing," Gupta said.

CHAPTER 2

Controversies About Food Allergies

Nut Allergy Is a Life-Threatening Condition That Needs to Be Taken Seriously

Robert A. Wood

Robert A. Wood is a member of the Food Allergy and Anaphylaxis Network's medical advisory board and director of pediatric allergy and immunology at the Johns Hopkins University School of Medicine. He is the author of *Food Allergies for Dummies.* In the following viewpoint Wood argues that food allergies are not a product of mass hysteria, as some claim, but instead are a serious and potentially deadly immune system disorder. He says that many children and adults die each year from anaphylactic shock brought on by food allergies and that the only reason more do not perish is because of the high degree of vigilance surrounding this life-threatening condition. According to Wood, claims that food allergies are exaggerated or affect only "rich, leftist communities" are inaccurate and insulting to those who suffer from the condition or have lost loved ones to a food allergy, which he says affects those from all communities and income levels.

Photo on facing page. Many say that most of the fear about allergies to nuts is a product of mass hysteria and that only one in five children tests positive for a peanut allergy. (© Arco Images GmbH/ Alamy)

Questions remain about the causes and recent increases in the number of children and adults with food allergies. The fact that such allergies are very common in the United States, Canada, Europe and other industrialized countries around the world, however, is undeniable. Contrary to what [*Los Angeles*] *Times* columnist Joel Stein wrote in his Jan. 9 [2009] Op-Ed column, "Nut allergies—a Yuppie invention," anaphylaxis is not brought on by the need for attention by "a parent who needs to feel special." Anaphylaxis is a serious allergic reaction that can be caused by exposure to minuscule quantities of nuts or other food allergens and may even cause death.

Food Allergies Are a Serious Immune System Response

The hives, swelling and severe breathing difficulty that people may experience during an allergic reaction are not symptoms of a "psychogenic [psychologically originated] illness," but rather an unbelievably frightening and dangerous response of the immune system to certain foods the body misinterprets as harmful. The fact is, food is the leading cause of anaphylaxis outside the hospital setting, and many children and adults die each year because they ate something they thought was safe. Once a reaction begins, no one knows how bad it will be, hence the worry and fear that is part of living with food allergies.

The scientific community is in agreement that more research funding is needed to answer why we see so much food allergy in young children today. We also need better treatment options. Currently, avoidance is the only way to prevent an allergic reaction for a true food allergy.

When you tell the parents of a child with a food allergy that their child could suffer, wind

FAST FACT

A 2011 study published in *Pediatrics* found that African American children have more than twice the rate of sensitivity to common allergen-containing foods compared with white children, with a particular vulnerability to peanut allergies.

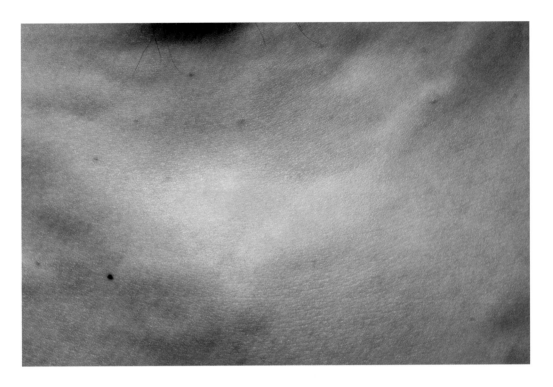

up in the hospital or worse unless they follow strict instructions from a doctor, you begin to understand why parents of children with food allergies are so vigilant. For those parents raising children with food allergies, educating others to take food allergies seriously is vital to preventing a reaction.

Stein says that food allergies kill about as many people a year as lightning strikes, suggesting that we therefore shouldn't take this medical condition seriously. The point he completely misses—or worse yet chooses to ignore—is that deaths are so infrequent *only* because of this high level of vigilance.

An anaphylactic rash. Anaphylaxis is a serious allergic reaction that is caused by exposure to small quantities of food allergens. (© **Medical-On-Line/Alamy**)

Vigilance and Anxiety: Appropriate Responses to a Real Danger

Even more disturbing is Stein's assertion—without a shred of evidence to support it—that "peanut allergies are only an issue in rich, leftist communities." Perhaps he

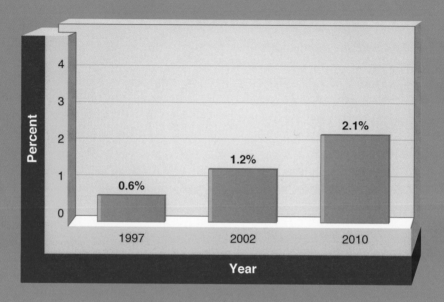

Prevalence of Peanut/Tree Nut Allergy for Children Under Eighteen

Taken from: Scott H. Sicherer et al. "US Prevalence of Self-Reported Peanut, Tree Nut, and Sesame Allergy: 11-Year Follow-Up." *The Journal of Allergy and Clinical Immunology*, vol. 125, no.6, June 2010, pp. 1322–1326. www.jacionline.org/article/50091–6749(10)00575–0/fulltext.

should speak to the parents of one of my former patients, an African American child from an inner-city area who died of a peanut reaction, to understand just how inaccurate and even hurtful that comment might be.

I care for more than 4,000 children with food allergies, nearly 2,000 of whom are allergic to peanuts and nuts. I myself have a lifelong, severe peanut allergy. If Stein were to spend a day in my clinic, he would quickly learn that food allergies are very real, truly dangerous and really do affect families of all races, ethnicities and socioeconomic strata. He would also learn that although food allergies do indeed cause anxiety, the anxiety is legitimate and that in spite of this anxiety, most families have an accurate perspective of the disease and practice a completely appropriate level of vigilance.

Food allergies are not a joke; they are a serious health condition. The concern with articles such as Stein's is that people will misunderstand food allergies and not take them seriously, putting many people at even greater risk. We have made tremendous strides in providing education about food allergy and we will continue to make progress in spite of Stein's insulting and inappropriate column.

IgG Allergy Tests Are Not Effective

Helen Branswell

Helen Branswell is the medical reporter for The Canadian Press, Canada's news agency, and a Nieman Global Health Fellow at Harvard University. In the following viewpoint Branswell presents the perspective of allergy specialist Dr. Elana Lavine, who argues that commercially available IgG (immunoglobulin G) tests, which are used by alternative-health practitioners to detect food allergies and sensitivities, are unreliable and do not correspond to what is known about how allergies work. According to Lavine, scientists do not know what an IgG immune response means but suspect it merely indicates that the body has been exposed to a particular protein. Scientifically verified allergy tests detect the presence of immunoglobulin E (IgE), known to be generated in response to a particular food allergen and indicative of a genuine allergic response. Lavine notes that immunology and allergy societies in the United States and Europe have stated that IgG testing is not valid for detecting food allergies.

Commercial tests that claim to determine whether a person has food allergies, sensitivities or an inability to tolerate certain foods are a waste of money, warns a Toronto allergy specialist, who wrote about the issue in [the March 19, 2012,] *Canadian Medical Association Journal.*

Elana Lavine said she's seeing a stream of people who have undergone the testing or have had it done on their children in the belief that a food allergy might explain other complaints or ailments. The tests are sometimes done in consultation with complementary medicine practitioners (such as naturopaths), she said.

Dr. Lavine said she hasn't been keeping records, but probably sees a couple of patients a month who want help interpreting the findings of the tests.

Immunoglobulin E (IgE) is an antibody in the blood that is involved in allergic reactions. The reaction makes the skin so sensitive that a rash forming "IgE" was produced simply by rubbing the skin with a finger containing the allergen. (© Dr. M.A. Ansary/Science Source)

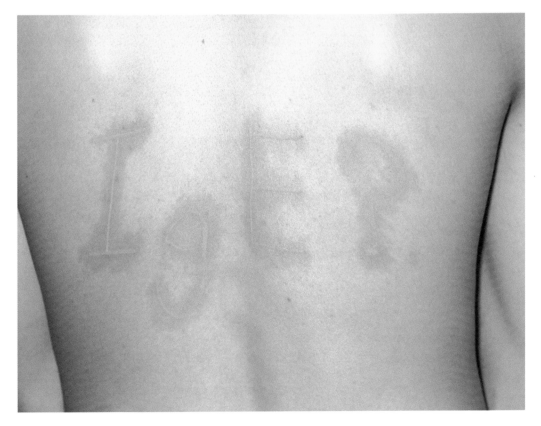

Immunoglobulin G (IgG) Tests

"I no longer have any preconceptions about the 'type of person' who would fall for this testing because of what I've seen in my community practice," said Dr. Lavine, an allergist who splits her time between a private practice and the pediatrics department of Humber River Regional Hospitals.

"I have seen well-intentioned, educated, aware people from all walks of life, all levels of education somehow be brought to a mindset where they feel like this test might be the answer.

For whatever reason, they're drawn to do a test that seems to promise to unlock secrets and to reveal to them what secret food allergies they have. So I think it's a very appealing concept—but a totally incorrect one," she said.

The tests, which can cost hundreds of dollars, look for an antibody reaction to a whole range of foods. And when they find a response with an antibody known as immunoglobulin G, or IgG, they characterize that result as unhealthy, suggesting the existence of either a food allergy, an intolerance or a food "sensitivity."

FAST FACT

According to the US Department of Health and Human Services, "Procedures for which there is no evidence of diagnostic validity include . . . food specific IgG, IgG4, and IgG/IgG4 antibody tests."

Inconsistent with Medical Science

But Dr. Lavine said that is a misreading of what an IgG reaction means. Science isn't 100 per cent sure what an IgG response actually signifies, she said, but it is thought to mean that a person has already encountered the proteins in that particular food and may even have developed a tolerance for them.

Recent position papers from European and U.S. allergy and immunology societies have also emphasized that tests looking at IgG or IgG4 antibodies are not appropriate for making a diagnosis of food allergy, she wrote in the journal.

Dr. Lavine noted that people who have undergone the testing may receive a multipage report that itemizes problem foods in unusual detail. A person might be told they have a sensitivity to cheddar cheese, cottage cheese and other cheese products.

Variation in IgG Test Results from Three Laboratories

Three laboratories were tested for consistency in immunoglobulin G (IgG) test results. For each lab, six blood samples were drawn from the same patient at the same time and sent for IgG testing. In the graph below, "numerical variance" is the average difference in the results between different (but equivalent) samples, while "clinical interpretation variance represents the average difference in clinical interpretation—i.e., for Lab A, the clinical interpretation for equivalent blood samples was different 59 percent of the time. Of the three labs tested, only Lab C had both numerical and clinical interpretation variances within accepted laboratory standards.

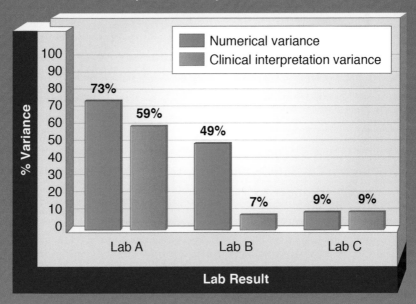

Taken from: Sheryl B. Miller. "IgG Food Allergy Testing by ELISA/EIA: What Do They Really Tell Us?" Townsend Letter, 1998. www.tldp.com/issue/174/IgG%20Food%20Allergy.html.

Dr. Lavine said that type of assessment is "inconsistent" with the understanding of food allergy, which identifies potential allergy-inducing components in dairy products, but would not list individual types of cheeses in this way. And some foods listed are actually rarely documented as allergens, such as sugar and yeast.

She also added there is no definition for a food "sensitivity."

How Allergy Testing Really Works

Taking blood samples and testing them against a large array of food proteins isn't the way food allergies are diagnosed, Dr. Lavine said.

Instead, a patient with a suspected food allergy—say someone who has developed hives or experienced difficulty swallowing or breathing after eating a particular food—would be referred by a primary-care doctor to an allergy specialist.

The allergy specialist would take a history and do a skin test, pricking the skin with a needle that had been dipped in an extract of the suspected allergen to see if a reaction—redness, itching or swelling—ensued. . . .

Sometimes allergists also order blood tests for specific allergens. . . . Those blood tests look for a response involving a different antibody—IgE [immunoglobulin E]—to a specific food or a small number of foods and cost in the $20 to $40 range per test, she said.

Dr. Lavine said she finds it particularly upsetting when she encounters a family with children grappling with the results of these tests.

[She said:] "In my practice, that's what's concerned me the most—seeing kids put onto restricted diets because of the results of these tests."

IgG Allergy Testing Is an Effective Medical Practice

Jason Bachewich

Jason Bachewich is a member of the Canadian Association of Naturopathic Doctors. In the following viewpoint he argues that medical doctors who claim that IgG (immunoglobulin G) testing is not effective do not understand how it really works. According to Bachewich, whereas IgE (immunoglobulin E) is generated immediately when the body has an immune response to a food allergen, IgG builds up in the body over time. If more builds up than the liver and kidneys can filter out, then "IgG complexes" will become embedded in tissues throughout the body and cause various health problems. The author says this is technically not an allergic reaction in the way that it is normally defined. Bachewich claims that because this mechanism works differently than the usual type of food allergic response, standard medical science does not yet recognize it as a valid disease process; nor does it recognize IgG tests as valid.

I am writing in response to the CBC [Canadian Broadcasting Corporation] news story [in March 2012] that went on a witch hunt for practitioners that use IgG [immunoglobulin G] Food Sensitivity testing. The story was completely biased towards the traditional medical views and the Naturopathic Doctor they interviewed for the story, in my opinion, has limited clinical experience. They also did not specify which tests and which companies they were referring to as these vary greatly in quality and consistency.

IgG allergy testing has numerous published human studies to show efficacy with asthma, headaches and indigestion. Clinical experience shows us that individuals with seemingly incurable psoriasis and eczema often benefit from the results of these tests. IBS [irritable bowel syndrome] and IBD [inflammatory bowel disease] also fall into this category, with hundreds of patients in our clinic alone being helped with the results of these tests.

IgG Testing Is Misunderstood

One of the arguments against this test is that it only picks up on foods you eat regularly. It is partly true. Your body will only make antibodies to antigens that it is exposed to. You will not be safe from Tetanus unless you have been exposed to the Tetanus vaccine. Therefore, if you are allergic to dairy but never eat dairy, then likely you will have no symptoms and will have no impetus to see a doctor or ask for the allergy testing. It is a moot point. . . .

IgG testing is a misunderstood phenomenon. IgE [immunoglobulin E] testing (skin prick), which is commonly understood as allergy testing, has a direct $1 + 1 = 2$ equation. IgE tests show an immediate and rapid response directly to the allergen ingested or breathed in. IgG is different. IgG complexes form, take 48–72 hours to completely peak and can last for

FAST FACT

Immunoglobulin G (IgG) is the smallest and most common antibody in the human immune system and plays an important role in fighting viral and bacterial infections.

months before dropping to normal levels. The reaction is completely different than an IgE test. It is not necessarily the type of allergen but the overall amount of antibody-antigen complexes. Think of it like this—IgE reactions are like a key and lock. If you have the right key, then the lock will open. A dairy protein will react to an IgE dairy antigen and you will have a swift and specific response.

A blood sample container is placed in an automated blood assay machine that analyzes the blood and ascertains its IgG levels. (© **CC Studio/ Science Source**)

How IgG Reactions Really Work

IgG reactions are like a dammed lake. The lake is the total amount of antibody-antigen complexes and the dam is the Liver and Kidneys. If the total amount of allergen complexes (no matter if it is from dairy, gluten, egg or anything else) builds up to a point where the dam can no longer hold it back, then it overflows. When it overflows (i.e. overwhelms the ability of the Liver and Kidneys to handle and filter the allergens), the allergen complexes then embed themselves in tissue throughout the body

Sample IgG (Immunoglobulin G) Test Results

IgG test results typically list many different food types, along with the magnitude of IgG reactivity to each one. These tests are highly controversial, and the meaning of the results is disputed.

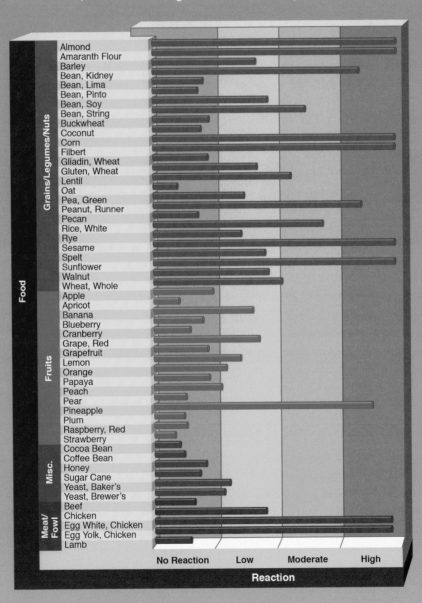

Taken from: Toni Kaste. "Order IgG Testing Direct to Your Door!" Lupus Hope, July 14, 2011.
http://lupushope.blogspot.com/2011/07/order-igg-testing-direct-to-you-door.html.

until the body can deal with it. If embedded in the skin you get psoriasis/eczema. If embedded in the lungs, you get asthma. These embedded complexes cause inflammation and irritation and do not allow the tissue to work properly. When the Liver and Kidneys catch up, the complexes are filtered and removed from the tissues and the symptoms decrease. Stress, lack of sleep and poor eating habits can all contribute to overloading the lake and the dam spills over.

So you can see that it is not as important with IgG testing to test the specific allergens but the overall allergen complex load. This is why it is technically not an allergen and the MD's [medical doctors] have an issue with it. If you have a hammer, then everything looks like nails. If you are trained in medical school to look at allergies in only one way then you can understand why they do not know what to do with this new science.

Just because a test procedure has not become mainstream, does not mean that it is not clinically beneficial. Diabetes used to be tested by tasting a patient's urine. You can imagine how many doctors picked up that test at the beginning too.

Genetic Engineering Can Produce Less-Allergenic Food Products

Food, Nutrition & Science from the Lempert Report

The following selection was taken from the website *Food, Nutrition & Science from the Lempert Report*, which is sponsored by Monsanto Company, a multinational chemical and agricultural biotechnology corporation. In the following viewpoint the authors argue that genetic engineering and related technology has the potential to reduce the allergenicity of food. This can be done either by creating new versions of food plants (e.g., peanuts) that lack genes that create specific allergens, or by using "gene silencing," a technique in which an allergen-producing gene is still present in the organism, but is "switched off," so that the gene will remain inactive and the allergen will not be present in the food. According to the authors, a study at Wageningen University in the Netherlands found that people are willing to accept genetically modified food if they believe it has strong benefits, such as a reduced tendency to cause allergic reactions.

Consumer attitudes toward genetically modified (GM) products could be more favorable when developed products deliver personally relevant benefits, according to a new study from Wageningen University in The Netherlands and published in *Food Quality and Preference* [in August 2010]. The study found that acceptance of GM as a process increased with increasing perceived personal benefits—in this case a reduction of allergic reactions to apples.

Reduced Allergenicity

In Northern Europe, where the study was conducted, apples are a major cause of food allergy among people that suffer from hay fever. When the Santana apple, a traditionally bred apple that has been identified as having a reduced allergenicity, was introduced as a hypoallergenic fruit in shops, researchers approached consumers with and without apple allergies. Consumers were asked to weigh the perceived personal health benefits and environmental benefits of genetically modified apples, as well as those grown with traditional breeding.

They found that consumer attitudes were significantly more positive toward those apples with greater benefits, like those bred to require fewer pesticides and those bred with greater hypoallergenicity. In fact, the higher the rate of allergy reduction, the higher the approval for the corresponding apples. For those that perceived allergy reduction after consumption of the Santana, they were more likely to feel positively about GM apples when the allergy reduction was closer to 95% than when the allergy reduction was closer to 66% or 5%.

Attitudes rated similarly toward the rate of pesticide reduction. Consumers were significantly more positive

> ## FAST FACT
>
> In 2012 Reuters reported that New Zealand researchers had created a genetically engineered cow that makes milk containing much less BLG, a protein that triggers an allergic reaction in susceptible children.

toward a 50% reduction in pesticides versus a 5% reduction, and those with a preference for organics were not impressed by a 5% reduction in pesticides. But all respondents, both those who preferred organics and those with a low preference for organics, rated a 50% reduction in pesticides equally.

Genetic Modification and "Gene Silencing"

"In our study pesticides were a control variable. We tried to include a case in which a technique has a benefit but not a personal benefit. Our results show that, in the 50% reduction case, everybody finds pesticide reduction important. Only when it is a small reduction (5%) did we detect differences between groups," says study co-author Dr. M. Schenk.

Within the GM methods, consumers reacted most favorably to apples bred with genes from another apple than they did to apples bred with genes from another plant. Overall, GM breeding was considered to be more acceptable if the participants received an individual benefit associated with the food. However, the majority of the consumers expressed a preference for the use of traditional breeding methods.

Sixty million Americans—that's one in four—have allergies or asthma. Currently, the only effective way of preventing allergic reactions is to eliminate the allergen from the diet. Genetic modification of foods is another method that could help prevent allergic reactions. While traditional methods of cross breeding could help to create a more hypoallergenic product, in this case apples, bringing a product like this to market could take up to 20 years. GM could help speed up the process. Also, the development of hypoallergenic foods by applying methods such as gene silencing, a method that is already being developed in soy, peanuts and tomatoes, could improve quality of life for food allergic consumers.

Acceptance of Genetic Modification

"As far as hypoallergenicity is concerned, we think that the first step should be to screen existing varieties of several fruit crops for their allergen content. Such screening may provide tools for breeders to include hypoallergenicity as

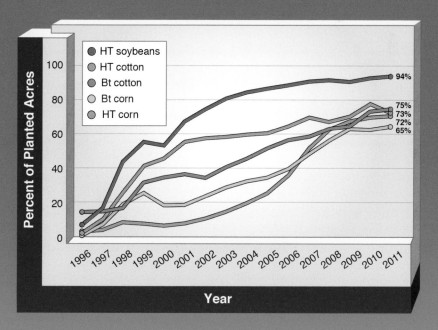

Growth in Adoption of Genetically Engineered Crops in the United States, 1996–2011

"HT" and "Bt" refer to different genetically engineered traits. "HT" means "herbicide tolerance," while "Bt" refers to crops that have been given genes from the soil bacterium *Bacillus thuringiensis*, causing them to produce a protein that kills lepidoptera larvae, an order of insects that includes butterflies and moths. 1996–1999 data are from a 2002 Agricultural Economic Report by Jorge Fernandez-Cornejo and William McBride. 2000–2011 data are from the US Department of Agriculture's National Agricultural Statistics Service and the Economic Research Service.

Taken from: Marion Nestle. "GM Crops in Crisis: Roundup-Resistant "Superweeds." Food Politics, May 14, 2012. www.foodpolitics.com/2012/05/gm-crops-in-crisis-roundup-resistant-superweeds/.

Giant chemical corporation Monsanto says that genetic engineering and related technologies have the potential to reduce the allergenicity of foods. (© Peter Newcomb/Bloomberg via Getty Images)

a target in their breeding program while developing future varieties. If peanut varieties can be produced minus the peanut allergens, this will reduce the level of antigens in general. Even though people who are allergic to peanuts may choose to avoid peanuts (as not all varieties are safe), their chance of accidental exposure will go down," says study co-author Dr. M. Smulders.

Smulders says that retailers can help by selling hypoallergenic variants and by supplying information to consumers to enable them to choose the product that best suits their needs—not only GM or non-GM, but also normal or hypoallergenic.

He adds, "Our results show that people do see GM as a technique that can provide benefits."

Schools Need to Be Safe and Inclusive Places for Children with Food Allergies

Kelly Rudnicki

Kelly Rudnicki is the mother of a child with multiple food allergies and the author of the *Food Allergy Mama* blog (www.foodallergymama .com). In the following viewpoint Rudnicki argues that schools need to be safe and inclusive spaces for everyone, including children with food allergies. Under section 504 of the Rehabilitation Act of 1973, federally funded institutions such as schools have a duty to accommodate children with disabilities, which includes food allergies. A "504 Plan" specifies precisely how the child's needs will be accommodated by the institution. According to Rudnicki, her son's new school did not follow her 504 Plan; for example, by notifying her when food treats would be served so that she could provide a safe alternative. As a result, in the first six weeks of school, three times her child could not participate in a school event that included treats. Rudnicki says schools need to do a better job of accommodating food allergies.

SOURCE: Kelly Rudnicki, "Rainbows, Hope and Maya Angelou," *The Food Allergy,* June 7, 2012. Copyright © 2012 by Kelly Rudnicki. All rights reserved. Reproduced by permission.

The past six weeks of adjusting my family of seven to a completely new way of life has been challenging to say the least. Though I *thought* I prepared fully for such a big move from the Midwest, a place I've lived my entire life, to the West Coast for my new life, I realized how mistaken I was. One can never prepare fully for leaving behind everything and everyone you know, just to follow what is inside your heart. Moving towns, let alone across the country with five young children, I've learned, isn't for the faint of heart. It is like having your first child; for as hard as you thought being a new parent was, it's 1000 times harder. I was prepared for the logistics of the move. But I wasn't prepared for all the other stuff, like completely starting from scratch when it came to my son's food allergies in school.

Schools Should Be Safe and Inclusive

Food allergy awareness and policy in schools is pretty much non-existent here, or at least where I live in So-Cal [Southern California]. Coming from a school district where I worked hard to make positive and healthy changes for kids with food allergies, I was stunned by the lack of protection for kids here. I was stunned by the amount of food, treats and parties being offered to kids in elementary and middle school. I was even more stunned that my son's new allergist said he's only helped about 4 food allergy families with drafting a Section 504 Plan to accommodate FA [food-allergic] children in their schools. Treats are often distributed, and the FA child sits the celebration out, repeatedly. I know, because this has happened to John three times already, and he's only been in this new school six weeks.

Even beyond the inclusion/exclusion issue, there is the whole safety issue of having a child around food that he/she could inadvertently eat or put into their mouth and have a potentially life-threatening reaction. I have used a great 504 Plan for several years now that specifically requests I am notified every time treats are brought into the classroom, so [that] a. I can send in an alternate treat, and b. to make sure whatever *is* brought in is Dairy and Nut Free. I was never notified in advance, which obviously is a huge problem for many reasons.

It's very simple: classrooms should be safe havens for all children, and every child deserves to feel included and safe in their classrooms, regardless of age or disability. Food allergies are a disability *not a choice*, and it's time more schools . . . take ownership of this fact and develop policies and procedures to reflect their commitment to keeping *all* children safe. There are too many gaping holes, gray areas, and room for error and potential for

The Rehabilitation Act of 1973 mandates that federally funded institutions, such as public schools, put in place a "504 plan," which specifies precisely how a child with allergies must be accommodated. (© AP Images/PRNews Foto/Food Allergy & Anaphylaxis Network)

miscommunication going on here as well as in schools across the country. As I said to my son's new allergist, there's a "perfect storm" brewing. . . . Something catastrophic can and will happen if these schools don't pull in the reins and develop guidelines for these kids. And they will be held liable, especially if that FA child has a 504 Plan.

An Inspiring Example

I've never considered myself an extremist, only a mom who cares not only about my child's health and well being at school, but *all* children at school. Nothing saddens me more than a child feeling alone, withdrawn, left out and anxious. No one deserves this, and kids with food allergies deserve better than that. They deserve the same respect and courtesy as any other kid. Again, this is a basic life lesson that everyone can learn from—love and take care of one another. Look out for one another. And respect each other. I don't want food bans; I just want policy and written clarification about what's acceptable and what's not. I want to know that my 504 Plan will be honored and followed to the letter. It's time for these schools to step up. . . .

I have *great* hope for what's ahead and believe . . . that at the end of the day, everyone is doing the best they can with what they have and what they know. [Writer] Maya Angelou famously said, "When you know better, you do better." Educate, teach, inspire and help spread the word about how to keep our FA kids safe, included and *happy*.

Finally, an amazing example of hope: My son's previous school in IL [Illinois] throws a huge 4th Grade Farewell party at the end of the school year, a right of passage for these kids going into 5th grade and middle school. The party is complete with a DJ, Bouncy House, and of course,

> ## FAST FACT
>
> The Food Allergy and Anaphylaxis Network reports that in 20–25 percent of occasions where epinephrine was administered in a school setting, the allergy was unknown prior to the incident.

Timing of Fatal Food-Induced Anaphylactic Reactions

In a study of six cases of fatal food-induced anaphylactic shock in children and adolescents, four of which occurred in a school setting, epinephrine was not given until long after the onset of symptoms, possibly contributing to the deaths. The study stresses that schools need to be prepared to treat allergic reactions to food promptly and effectively.

Patient No.	Setting	Initial Onset of Symptoms	Time of Epinephrine Dose	Onset of Severe Symptoms	Type of Symptoms	Time of Death
		minutes after ingestion				
1	School	10	125	125	Gastrointestinal, respiratory	180
2	School*	20	80	65	Gastrointestinal, respiratory	95
3	School	20	180	150	Gastrointestinal, respiratory	300
4	Fair	30	60	35	Skin, respiratory	105
5	School	30	90	35 & 100**	Gastrointestinal, respiratory	240
6	Home	3	25	20	Gastrointestinal, respiratory	120

*The symptoms began at home.
**The severe symptoms subsided after treatment with supplemental oxygen and then recurred.

Taken from: Hugh A. Sampson et al. "Fatal and Near-Fatal Anaphylactic Reaction to Food in Children and Adolescents." *New England Journal of Medicine*, vol. 327, pp. 380–384, August 6, 1992. www.nejm.org/doi/full/10.1056/NEJM199208063270603#t=article.

food. This year [2012], the food committee went out of their way to bring in fun, kid-friendly food that *everyone* could enjoy. No one was left out, regardless of their dietary needs. How amazing is that? My friend sent me photos of kids eating hot dogs, chips and cotton candy, but vendors and products were checked and double checked. It was beautiful, and brought me to tears as I showed John the photos of all his old friends eating food that he would have been able to eat, too. He was really happy for them, and thought it was really cool that these moms cared enough to think of kids like him. It blew me away, to be honest, because that kind of compassion and care for accommodating all the kids is nothing short of spectacular. And it's a reminder that, as I've always said, "Anything Is Possible." A *huge* thank you to all those amazing parents in IL, and everywhere, for keeping that message of hope alive, and for taking such good care of our children. And never, ever give up hope.

Nothing to Sneeze at: Allergies May Be Good for You

Melinda Wenner Moyer

Melinda Wenner Moyer is a science and health writer based in Brooklyn, New York, and the author of the blog *Body Politic: Investigating Drugs, Foods, and Chemicals*. In 2010 she won the American College of Emergency Physicians Journalism Award. In the following viewpoint Moyer reports on a controversial food-allergy theory proposed by an immunobiologist at Yale University named Ruslan Medzhitov. Medzhitov claims that allergies are a protective mechanism that the body evolved to protect people from harmful substances by either expelling them from the body or by motivating people to avoid the unpleasant symptoms associated with them. He says that allergic symptoms such as runny nose, sneezing, and coughing work to remove material (such as an ingested allergen) from the body. According to Medzhitov, these protective mechanisms can in some cases be dangerously excessive and may falsely label something safe as dangerous, for example, if it was consumed in a polluted environment.

Ah, glorious springtime. It brings flowers, warmer temperatures—and for many, incessant sneezes and sniffles. Everybody curses allergies as annoying at best, and some allergic reactions—such as anaphylaxis, which rapidly lowers blood pressure and closes the airways—can be fatal. But a handful of researchers now propose that allergies may actually have evolved to protect us. Runny noses, coughs and itchy rashes keep toxic chemicals out of our bodies, they argue, and persuade us to steer clear of dangerous environments.

Most immunologists consider allergies to be misdirected immune reactions to innocuous substances such as pollen or peanuts. Viral and bacterial infections invoke what are called "type 1" immune responses, whereas allergies involve "type 2" responses, which are thought to have evolved to protect against large parasites. Type 1 responses directly kill the pathogens and the human cells they infect; type 2 works by strengthening the body's protective barriers and promoting pest expulsion. The idea is that smaller pathogens can be offensively attacked and killed, but it's smarter to fight larger ones defensively.

But Ruslan Medzhitov, an immunobiologist at Yale University, has never accepted the idea of allergies as rogue soldiers from the body's parasite-fighting army. Parasites and the substances that trigger allergies, called allergens, "share nothing in common," he says—first, there are an almost unlimited number of allergens. Second, allergic responses can be extremely fast—on the scale of seconds—and "a response to parasites doesn't have to be that fast," he says.

In a paper published April 26 in *Nature*, Medzhitov and his colleagues argue that allergies are triggered by potentially dangerous substances in the environment or food to protect us. (*Scientific American* is part of Nature

FAST FACT

A 2011 study published in *Cancer Epidemiology, Biomarkers & Prevention* found that the more allergies people have, the less likely they are to develop glioma (a type of brain cancer).

Publishing Group.) As evidence, they cite research including a 2006 study published in *The Journal of Clinical Investigation* reporting that key cells involved in allergic responses degrade and detoxify snake and bee venom. A 2010 study published in the same journal suggests that allergic responses to tick saliva prevent the pests from attaching and feeding. This mechanism, he argues, is distinct from the classic type 2 response the body uses to defend itself against internal parasites.

More generally, hated allergic symptoms keep unhealthy environmental irritants out of the body, Medzhitov posits. "How do you defend against something you inhale that you don't want? You make mucus. You make a runny nose, you sneeze, you cough, and so forth. Or if it's on your skin, by inducing itching, you avoid it or you try to remove it by scratching it," he explains. Likewise, if you've ingested something allergenic, your body might

Some researchers now propose that allergies may actually have evolved to protect us. They argue that runny noses, coughs, and itchy rashes are the body's way of ridding itself of toxic chemicals. (© Ian West/Alamy)

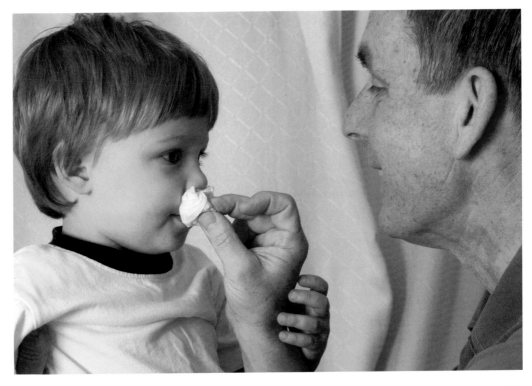

react with vomiting. Finally, if a particular place or circumstance ramps up your allergies, you're likely to avoid it in the future. "The thing about allergies is that as soon as you stop exposure to an allergen, all the symptoms are gone," he says.

Importantly, Medzhitov notes that although allergies are intended to be helpful, they *are* sometimes excessive and detrimental—the body can go too far. And allergies don't always make sense. "I would say that food is still mostly innocuous," says Dale Umetsu, an immunologist at Children's Hospital Boston, yet "food allergies affect one in 12 kids." How is that protective? According to Medzhitov, foods may have proteins in them that are harmful or they might mimic potentially harmful substances. (With food, he says, there's often little consensus about what, exactly, the offending allergen is.) And one has to think of the evolutionary past, he adds: for our ancestors hundreds of thousands of years ago, many plants that looked like food *were* toxic, so allergies may have evolved to protect us from them. Finally, he says that some allergies may develop through a "guilt by association" mechanism: An individual might develop an egg allergy after eating eggs in a polluted environment, for instance. "This is a type of detection by proxy—you use some cue, like smell, or a visual cue or taste, to indicate if

Positive Food-Allergy Side Effects

Positive food-allergy side effects may include:
• Healthier eating habits
• Improved baking skills
• Increased number of meals together at the dinner table

Taken from: "Side Effects—Food Allergy Cartoon." *Food Allergy Fun,* July 22, 2012. http://foodallergyfun.blogspot.com/2012/07/side-effects-food-allergy-cartoon.html.

a food is associated with something that's noxious. Next time you're exposed to it, you avoid it."

This still doesn't explain why some people are more allergy-prone than others. "Allergens are everywhere," says Erika von Mutius, an allergy specialist at Munich University Children's Hospital in Germany. "So if this is a defense, why isn't everybody allergic?" According to Medzhitov, allergies may be more common in people with defects in other defensive tactics. For instance, 42 percent of people who have a mutation in a structural skin protein called filaggrin commonly experience allergic skin reactions. "If you don't have optimal physical barriers, you rely on a greater degree on allergic defenses," he says.

And what about the growing body of research suggesting that childhood environment shapes allergy risk? A 2011 study published in *The New England Journal of Medicine* reported that children who grow up on farms, where they are exposed to many microorganisms, are less likely than other kids to develop asthma and allergies. This idea, known as the hygiene hypothesis, suggests that individuals who encounter a multitude of bacteria and viruses early in life invest more immune resources into type 1 responses at the cost of type 2 reactions, including allergies. Medzhitov maintains that this theory can co-exist with his own. "It's a different aspect of disease susceptibility that has to do with early programming," he says.

Ultimately, Medzhitov's theory raises more questions than it answers, but many agree that the basic tenets are plausible. "It stimulates us as scientists to draw up some new hypotheses," says Kari Nadeau, an immunologist at the Stanford School of Medicine. "The hypotheses need to be tested and might not necessarily be confirmed, but at least this paper drives us to understand allergies better."

CHAPTER 3

Personal Experiences with Food Allergies

An Allergy Doctor Describes Her Experience as the Mother of Three Food-Allergic Children

Sarah M. Boudreau-Romano

Sarah M. Boudreau-Romano is a pediatrician and allergist with three food-allergic children. The following selection is from a speech she gave at the Food Allergy Initiative's (FAI's) Fourth Annual Chicago Benefit in 2011. Boudreau-Romano shares how it felt for her as a professional allergist to discover that she was also the mother of three children with very serious allergies to many different foods. The author describes in detail two serious medical crises her children experienced: one in which her son nearly died after eating a cookie she thought was safe and another case in which her daughter went into anaphylactic shock after drinking baby formula made from cow's milk.

I started my first year of Allergy/Immunology fellowship in 2005. We had a brand new baby boy at home. Before I *ended* my first year of fellowship, we had three baby boys at home! If having 3 kids in 13 months wasn't enough to make the remainder of my fellowship a

Photo on facing page. According to the Centers for Disease Control and Prevention, about 3 million children below the age of eighteen in the United States have allergies. (© Andrew Fox/Alamy)

SOURCE: Sarah M. Boudreau-Romano, "Let Me Introduce Myself…" *The Allergist Mom*, October 25, 2011. Copyright © 2011 by Sarah M. Bourdreau-Romano. All rights reserved. Reproduced by permission.

challenge, one of the boys, Gino, was showing early signs of allergic disease. He had terrible eczema that kept him up crying and scratching most nights, he would get hives constantly, and he vomited every single time he ate.

After months of denial, I finally had Gino tested for cow's milk allergy. As the diagnosis fell from my allergist's lips, the same diagnosis that so often fell from mine, it struck me how it felt on the other side and the strike was powerful. The very field I was preparing to dedicate my whole life to was betraying me. That was the moment when the tables turned on me. I was on the wrong side of that appointment, a side I never dreamed I would be on. I was not the allergist that day; I instead became the mother of a child with food allergy.

Soon thereafter, I would become the mother of not only one but *three* children with life-threatening food allergies to multiple different foods, including milk, egg, soy, wheat, green pea, beans, mustard, sesame, peanut, tree nuts, chicken, fish, shellfish, red grape, cranberry and banana. It probably would have been easier to tell you what they can eat!

I would like to share two stories with you that highlight the seriousness of allergic disease, the unexpected nature of reactions, the ultimate importance of epinephrine and the incredible need for a cure.

Almost Killed by a Cookie

I remember it was a pretty summer afternoon and I was on call so my mom, dad and sister, who are an incessant support to us, stopped by to help. I was so excited to see the boys when I got home from work [that] I let them eat dessert before dinner. I gave them each a tiny bite of a milk-free, wheat-free cookie I had made the night before. It was not even a minute after their first glorious bite when my mom nervously brought to my attention that Milo's lips and eyes were swelling and he had hives around his mouth. My heart sunk fast. I grabbed some Benadryl® and as I gave him a dose, my dad yelled out my name, and he said it in such a way that I knew something horrible was happening. Gino was lying still on the floor. My dad picked him up and ran over to me. When he handed him to me, I felt his weight. That is the strongest memory I have of that moment, his weight. He wasn't holding any of it on his own, he was completely limp in my arms and when I sat him up and screamed his name to get him to look at me, his head just slumped forward heavy against my chest.

He began to look dusky and blue around his lips. I screamed for an Epipen, Jr® [epinephrine autoinjector for small children]. And even though I can put teeny tiny umbilical lines into two pound babies without so much

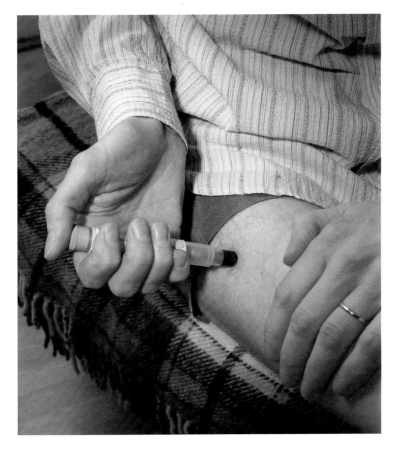

Sarah promptly injected epinephrine into her son—as this person is doing here—when he had a violent, life-threatening reaction to a cookie, probably saving his life. (© Papa Kay/Alamy)

as a tremor in my fingers, with my own child, I was shaking so much that I could hardly remove the gigantic gray cap from the Epipen, Jr®. When I finally did, I put it into his thigh with a thud. While I counted to ten, he began vomiting profusely. His nose was bubbling out mucus, and he was turning more and more blue. I could feel myself losing him and I believed that he might be dying in my arms. Dying from a cookie that most of the world would find nothing but joy in. *Dying from a cookie.* Specifically dying from the egg in that cookie. A few minutes after the injection of epinephrine, his coloring began to return and I felt this overwhelming sense of relief and gratitude as he started to open his eyes again. That night in the hospital I remember crying and clutching to Gino for dear life and thanking God that I could.

FAST FACT

A 2012 article in the *Wall Street Journal* reports that since 2002 the number of Americans with an EpiPen has increased by 72 percent to 1.8 million; 46 percent of users are children.

Another Medical Crisis

We have unfortunately had many similar reactions to food in the past five years. Most recently our baby, Lucy, had anaphylaxis within 30 seconds of drinking her first ounce of cow's milk–based formula at 4 months old. Her face began to swell almost immediately. She was retching and coughing. My ever-smiling baby was growing distant and weak. She was too small for an Epipen, Jr® so I immediately called 911. When we got to the ER [emergency room], she began to have more difficulty swallowing and she was starting to drool.

The underside of her tongue was so swollen that it looked like she had two tongues, one stacked on top of the other and the back of her throat was beginning to swell so she had just a narrow passage through which air could flow. Two injections of epinephrine later, she started to look better, the swelling was going down and I could actually get her to smile and when she finally did smile, that was a smile I will never ever forget. It was a smile that brought us *both* back to life.

I share these stories to demonstrate the urgency that [my husband] D.J. and I have to find the treatment for food allergy. We are not alone in this urgency; we are in the company of millions of other people. We want Gino to be able to eat the pizza at his friend's birthday parties. We want Milo to be able to eat a doughnut in the morning when he spends the night at my parents' house. We want Lucy to be able to eat cheese to her heart's content. We want Sal, our son without food allergy, to be able to share these experiences with his brothers and sister and by doing so, he will be able to carry less worry and less burden. We want a treatment for this disease so that all people with food allergy can eat *what* they want, *when* they want, *wherever* they want without the fear of having a fatal reaction. That is their reality and it is a reality that desperately needs to change.

Losing a Child to Food Allergies

Paul and Catrina Vonder Meulen

Paul and Catrina Vonder Meulen lost their daughter Emily to a fatal anaphylactic shock when she was thirteen years old. In the following selection, they describe in detail what happened that day, as well as how the false sense of security they had about their child's food allergy contributed to her death. The Vonder Meulens share the lessons they learned and what they wish they had known before their daughter had her fatal reaction.

When Emily was about two years old, Paul gave her a peanut butter cracker, almost immediately she started to fuss and rub at her eyes and start to develop hives. He gave her Benadryl and the allergic reaction calmed down. It was only after Emily's death and subsequent research that Paul realized that this was when Emily's immune system started building antibodies to fight off [an allergy to] nuts.

SOURCE: Paul and Catrina Vonder Meulen, "Emily's Story and Our Message," FoodallergyAngel.com. Copyright © Emily Vonder Meuler Memorial Fund. All rights reserved. Reproduced by permission.

After this initial exposure to nuts, Emily's body developed its own protective warning system. If she came in contact with a food that had been exposed to nuts, she would have a tingling sensation on the back of her tongue, she would immediately spit the food out and then to protect itself, her body would vomit trying to expel whatever the offending allergen was. It was that reaction that made us comfortable with this allergy. She knew what she could and couldn't eat. If kids brought snacks into school and they couldn't tell her if it had nuts in it or not, she wouldn't eat it. If they said it was free of nuts, she would still test it by putting it to her lips and touching it with her tongue. If she didn't have a reaction, she knew it was safe.

A Fatal Reaction

I think you really want to know more of what happened that day, but I needed to let you know why I was so unprepared for what happened on April 13th [2006]. Elena (10), Emily and I had gone shopping that day for a graduation dress at a mall here in Cincinnati. After buying her dress (which she wore out of the store) we stopped to have lunch at about 2:50 at the mall's food court. We decided to have a sandwich at a place that we had eaten before (we considered it a "safe food" restaurant) because Emily, in fact, had eaten this very same sandwich many times before with no problems. Their website even shows that it is peanut-free except for two of their cookies. After having lunch, we walked through a new t-shirt shop where Emily fell, tripping over her shoes, and landing on her bottom. She laughed and got right back up. We continued shopping, going to a store where we were going to get Emily's ears pierced. While we were in this shop, Emily mentioned that she was afraid she might have messed her underwear when she fell and wanted to check it out. She came back about 5 minutes later, did two puffs of her inhaler, telling me that she felt hot and did her face look red. I told her no, but maybe we should leave. She said that her new dress felt tight and that she wanted to change her clothes. I said fine. She took her clothes and went to the bathroom. Elena and I stayed at the shop looking at "girly" stuff.

A few minutes later, I got a phone call from a girl in the bathroom asking if I have a daughter Emily and that she was having trouble breathing. Elena and I rushed to the bathroom where we found Emily gasping for air. She tried to do her inhaler again, but I could tell from looking at her that this was not good. The whites of her eyes were completely red and her normally pink cheeks were white. I immediately called 911. Emily had enough air to ask two questions. Emily became disoriented and wandered into the hallway. I had her lay down and she passed out. A woman passing by and I started performing CPR [cardiopulmonary resuscitation] while Elena was on the phone with 911. The woman that was helping me said that Emily was O.K., and another woman said she felt air coming out of her nose. To me, Emily was not O.K., she was blue. Then I heard the strangest sound come out her mouth. People later told me it was her death-breath. 911 had not shown up yet. Emily was taken to the hospital where they continued CPR. I arrived maybe 10 minutes later where the doctors told me they could not get her heart to start. They had finally got the breathing tube in the right spot, but they had given her all the medicine they are allowed to jumpstart her heart plus more, with no success. They were telling me my daughter was dead. It was 4:20. I believe Emily passed away in the bathroom hallway at the mall, which would have been around 3:45.

FAST FACT

The Food Allergy and Anaphylaxis Network reports that food from a restaurant or other food service establishment causes almost half of food allergy reactions that result in death.

A False Sense of Security

To answer your questions:

Did she have an Epi Pen [epinephrine autoinjector] with her? If so . . . was it administered immediately?

NO, I did not have an Epi-pen with me. Unfortunately, if I did have an Epi-pen with me, I don't know if I would have known to use it. I thought Emily was having an asthma attack because of her fall. I didn't know that what was happening to her was associated with food. She didn't have the tingling on her tongue, she didn't vomit, it was a safe food (so we thought).

What did she have to eat at the Deli?

Emily had the Sweet Onion Chicken-Teriyaki Wrap. We knew it contained soy sauce. This particular deli did not make peanut butter and jelly sandwiches. We still don't know where the trace amount of peanut came from. Unfortunately, the coroner and the investigator can't prove anything at this moment, but because her reaction was so rapid and violent, the coroner has no other option but to point to the last meal Emily ate. Somehow a trace amount of peanut cross contaminated the sandwich she had eaten. We are still waiting for lab results—until then the findings are inconclusive.

How quick was her reaction?

We ordered around 2:50 and were done eating about 3:10. My best guess is that around 3:20 is when she started feeling hot and went to change her clothes. I called 911 at 3:26 and I believe she was gone around 3:40. The [doctors] pronounced her dead at 4:20.

Did she have any close calls before her death from reactions to something she had eaten?

NO, she did not have any close calls before this incident. Paul and I were in a comfort zone counting on Emily's internal alarm system and the fact that she knew what she could and couldn't eat, while we were blind to the fact that she was still very much in danger. Please understand, Emily was terrified of the Epi-pen and was diligent about asking questions about food preparation and ingredients. She did not want to be stuck with the Epi-pen. That's what makes this all the harder to understand, Emily was her own advocate.

Lessons Learned

Your child is at a wonderful age, you can still control what they eat, you are watchful to make sure they don't put the wrong thing in their mouth, you are their advocate. During this age, you can learn what the symptoms of anaphylactic shock are, you can develop a plan in case of an emergency, and go over and over what the plan is with friends and family so, God forbid, that emergency comes, you don't think, you react.

As your child gets older, and they become more independent and responsible, don't relax! According to FAAN [Food Allergy and Anaphylaxis Network], children between the ages of 10 and 19 are at a much higher risk of fatality. It defies logic, because you think now your child is at an age where they know and understand the dangers of their allergies and they will not take a chance. But what you don't know or think you know is what can take their life so quickly. It is almost as if every time you eat prepared food, your child has a gun pointed at their

Emily's mother did not have an EpiPen with her when Emily experienced a fatal allergic reaction. She is not sure one would have saved Emily's life anyway. (© Medical-On-Line/Alamy)

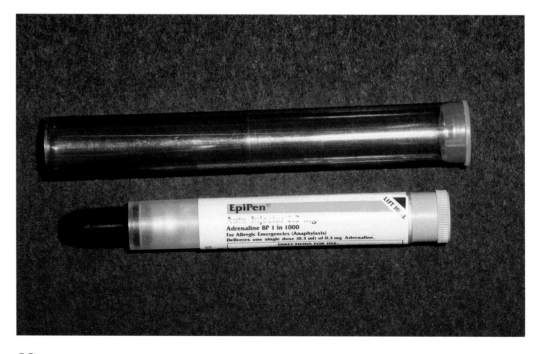

heart. We don't want to scare parents, but we want you to be scared, so that you stay vigilant in protecting your child.

I know this may sound irresponsible but please read it for what it is, learning lessons. As a learning lesson, my family would eat shelled peanuts on the couch. When they were done, Emily and I would go into the living room and vacuum the couch and the carpets. I wanted her to understand that she has to protect herself and that she can't count on others to be as diligent as she had to be. Another time, we were taking a flight to San Diego. At the time, they still served peanuts on the plane. I had Emily wipe down the fold-down tray and arm rests in case the person who sat there before her ate peanuts and the residue remained on the surface.

The most bizarre part of this past 14 years is that I don't think I understood that Emily could die. I thought she would get hives, swelling, asthma attacks, or really sick, but never in all of my thoughts did I ever think of death. Why didn't that ever cross my mind? Did I not want to think that was a possibility? I now look at a lifetime of guilt, wondering how I could have done more. Please don't ever feel you are being too protective when it comes to the health of your child and if someone tells you to relax, tell them Emily's Story.

A Mother Puts Her Child's Food-Allergic Condition in Perspective

Kelley J.P. Lindberg

Kelley J.P. Lindberg is the mother of a young child with a peanut and tree-nut allergy. In the following selection Lindberg talks about her concerns with the difficulties and dangers her child will likely experience in school. When she visits a hospital with her child so that he can get an allergy test done, she sees many other children with far worse problems and realizes that, in comparison, she and her child are very fortunate.

My very good friend Shari once told me about an old Jewish proverb—something about how if we could all put our troubles in a bag and set it on a table, and then pick up someone else's bag, we'd choose our own again.

Funny how often I think about that.

When my son was 4, we'd already known about his peanut/nut allergy for a couple of years. I was having him retested to see if—against the odds—he'd outgrown it. With kindergarten looming (okay, so it was still a year and a half away—I like to get a head-start on my worrying), I was feeling sorry for myself, wondering why my son had to be cursed with a food allergy that would make normal school lunches anything but normal. How would I keep other kids from rubbing their PB&Js [peanut butter and jelly sandwiches] in his hair? What would I do if the teacher insisted all the students make ladybugs out of walnut shells? What if my son got tired of salami sandwiches? O, woe is me!!!

A little over the top, I admit.

Visiting the Hospital

To get his blood drawn for the allergy test, we went to a nearby hospital. It happens to be a renowned children's hospital, with the expertise and facilities that draw young patients from across the western U.S.

As we walked down the hall looking for the out-patient lab, we began passing some of those patients and their parents. There were children in wheelchairs, their bodies crumpled and contorted. There were children on gurneys, hooked up to machines that made sure their hearts kept beating or their lungs kept filling with air. There were children with bright smiles and missing limbs, and others with body parts intact, but a glazed-over look to their eyes that belied other damage.

Meanwhile, my 4-year-old whirlwind was running down the hall, shouting excitedly about the primary-colored mechanical water sculpture in the next lobby. As I tried to keep him from clambering into the fountain or hopping across the benches, I felt like I should be apologizing to all the other parents. This was a place for terribly sick children, I thought to myself. My child wasn't sick—he just had food allergies!

> **FAST FACT**
>
> According to the Centers for Disease Control and Prevention, in 2007 about 3 million children under eighteen years old had a digestive problem or food allergy.

A New Perspective

And just like that, my perspective reset itself. All my self-pity was transformed into a sense of shame, and my own bushel-bag of burdens began to look snack-sized.

What had I been whining about? My kid could run, laugh, climb, and get into a thousand varieties of trouble—all before breakfast! So what if I have to be extra careful about the breakfast he comes into contact with? So what if I have to carry an EpiPen [epinephrine auto-injector]? I and my son have the very good fortune to be living in an age when we have EpiPens, knowledgeable doctors, and an amazing variety of safe foods to choose from.

A few minutes later, my son was asking the nurse a dozen questions about drawing blood, and he watched, fascinated, as she drew his. His sharp little mind was so busy figuring out how the needle and tube worked that he forgot to cry. All the way out the door, he chattered

A young boy undergoes a pin-prick test for allergen screening. Lindberg's son had to endure many such tests. (© Burger/Phanie/ Science Source)

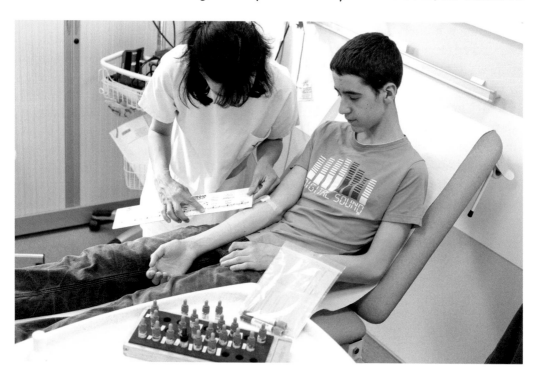

about how the next time I needed blood drawn, he could do it for me.

As we stepped out into the sunshine, I tucked my bag of troubles into my pocket. It felt familiar and—while not quite comfortable—a lot lighter.

Now, whenever someone new says, "Oh, dealing with his allergies must be terrible!" I try to imagine what might be lurking inside their bag of troubles. Then I shake my head, smile, and say, "As challenges go, I'll keep this one, thanks."

GLOSSARY

adrenaline   *See* **epinephrine.**

allergen   Any substance that can cause an allergic reaction.

allergenicity   The degree to which a substance has the effect of an allergen; a food with low allergenicity is said to be hypoallergenic.

allergist   A physician specializing in diagnosing and treating allergies, asthma, and related disorders of the immune system.

anaphylactic shock   *See* **anaphylaxis.**

anaphylaxis   A rapid, severe, and life-threatening physiological reaction to an antigen (e.g., a food protein), with symptoms such as hives, swelling, difficulty breathing, flushed skin, and loss of consciousness. Requires immediate medical attention.

antigen   Any substance, such as pollen, viruses, bacteria, or food proteins, that causes the body's immune system to produce antibodies against it.

antihistamine   A drug used to treat allergic reactions by blocking the effects of histamine.

atopy patch testing (APT)   A test in which suspected allergens are held in place on the skin for forty-eight hours, then observed in the days following removal to see whether a delayed reaction occurs. Used to test for cell-mediated reactions.

basophil   A type of white blood cell involved in allergic inflammation reactions.

cell-mediated   A condition in which the immune system reacts adversely to a food allergen but not by generating antibodies.

cross-contamination	When an allergen is transferred through contact from one food to another, causing the second food to become contaminated and unsafe for someone with a particular allergy.
cross-reactivity	When an allergic reaction originally triggered by one food is subsequently triggered by similar food; e.g., someone who developed an allergic reaction in response to an antigen present in lobster might experience an allergic reaction when exposed to shrimp.
elimination diet	A technique for identifying foods causing an allergic reaction in which all foods believed to be possible triggers are eliminated from the diet for a period of time, then gradually reintroduced one by one to see whether there is an allergic reaction.
epinephrine	A hormone secreted by the adrenal glands in response to stress, epinephrine dilates air passages, contracts blood vessels, and increases heart rate. Used to treat anaphylactic shock. Often called adrenaline.
epinephrine autoinjector	A device used to administer epinephrine to treat a severe allergic reaction.
EpiPen	A brand name of an epinephrine autoinjector.
food allergy	A condition in which the immune system mistakenly reacts to a benign food as if it were a harmful invader.
food hypersensitivity	*See* **food allergy.**
food intolerance	An adverse reaction to food that does not involve an immune system reaction; often confused with food allergy but much less likely to produce severe symptoms.
food protein–induced enterocolitis syndrome (FPIES)	An immune system reaction to common foods that occurs in some infants. FPIES is non-immunoglobulin E–mediated and is believed to be cell-mediated.
histamine	A substance released by cells during an allergic reaction that causes swelling and inflammation, leading to symptoms ranging from unpleasant to life threatening.

hives	Round, red, itchy welts on the skin that may occur during a food-allergy reaction. The technical medical term is *urticaria*.
hypoallergenic	Food products that are unlikely to trigger an allergic reaction.
IgE-mediated reactions	An allergic reaction that involves the body's generation of the antibody immunoglobulin E (IgE).
immunoglobulin E (IgE)	A type of antibody that recognizes allergens and triggers an allergic reaction.
immunoglobulin G (IgG)	The most common type of antibody, it is triggered by invasive organisms such as bacteria, viruses, and fungi.
mast cells	An immune system cell containing histamine and other substances that are released during allergic reactions.
medical-alert bracelet	A bracelet worn by a person with a life-threatening medical condition, such as food allergy, concisely explaining the condition in case the individual is incapacitated or otherwise incapable of explaining what is wrong when an attack occurs.
oral allergy syndrome (OAS)	A condition in which someone who has an allergy to a type of pollen experiences cross-reactivity to foods containing a protein that is similar to the allergen in that pollen; e.g., a person with a grass allergy may react to celery, tomatoes, peaches, melons, or oranges.
oral food challenge (OFC)	A food-allergy test in which the patient eats foods suspected of causing an allergic reaction. It is considered very reliable but must be done under medical supervision as it can cause a dangerous reaction.
oral immunotherapy	A risky experimental treatment in which gradually increasing doses of an allergen are orally administered to patients who are allergic to it, with the aim of desensitizing them to the substance and reducing their reaction.
patch test	An allergy test in which possible allergens are placed on the skin to see whether an allergic reaction takes place.

radioallergosorbent test	*See* RAST test.
RAST test	Short for radioallergosorbent test, it is used to help diagnose food allergies.
serum IgE test	A blood test that measures the levels of immunoglobulin E (IgE) in the blood.
skin prick test (SPT)	A test in which the skin is scratched and a liquid containing a common allergen is applied to see whether a reaction occurs.
skin test	A food-allergy test in which a substance is placed on, or injected into, the skin to see whether a reaction occurs.
urticaria	*See* **hives.**

CHRONOLOGY

6th–4th centuries B.C.	The Hippocratic Corpus notes that foods safe for some people can harm others: "Cheese does not harm all men alike, some can eat their fill of it, while others come off badly."
1st century A.D.	Roman philosopher and poet Lucretius notes that "what is food for some may be fierce poison for others."
1656	French chemist Pierre Borel performs the first skin test for food allergy when he puts egg on a patient's skin to show that the patient has an egg sensitivity.
1698	English physician Sir John Floyer, in *A Treatise of the Asthma*, lists exposures that worsen symptoms in his asthmatic patients: eggs, cheese, and oysters.
1808	Dr. Robert Villian vividly describes an allergic reaction to almonds in his patient, English physician Thomas Winterbottom.
1839	One of the first people to observe anaphylaxis, French physiologist François Magendie discovers that rabbits who tolerated an initial injection of egg albumin frequently died when later given a second injection.
1902	French physiologist Charles Richet notes that animals given a second injection of a foreign protein quickly died, despite not being harmed by the initial injection; he coins the term *anaphylaxis* to describe the condition.

1905   German doctors use what is today called oral immuno-therapy to desensitize infants with cow's milk allergy.

1906   Austrian doctor Clemens von Pirquet publishes his paper *Allergie*, coining the term *allergie/allergy* based on Greek *allos* (other) and *ergon* (work). Pirquet speculates that the diverse symptoms of allergy are a coordinated immune system reaction.

1911   Allergists Leonard Noon and John Freeman pioneer the use of allergy immunotherapy using injections of gradually increasing doses of an allergen extract.

1912   Oscar Schloss, a pediatrician in New York, publishes a paper in which he describes using oral desensitization to reduce a child's dangerous egg allergy to the point where the child could safely eat eggs.

1913   Richet is awarded the Nobel Prize in Physiology or Medicine for his anaphylaxis research.

1920s   The terms *allergy* and *anaphylaxis* are both being used in scholarly works. Gradually the former is used more commonly in public discourse.

1921   German scientists Carl Prausnitz and Heinz Kustner demonstrate the existence of a tissue-sensitizing substance associated with food-allergic reactions and suggest the term *reagin* (which later turns out to be immunoglobulin E), although they were not able to isolate the substance.

1929   The *Journal of Allergy*, the influential journal of the American Academy of Allergy, Asthma, and Immunology, is established. Later it would change its name to the *Journal of Allergy and Clinical Immunology*.

1940s   St. Mary's Allergy Clinic, the first official clinic specializing in allergy treatment, is founded in London, England, by John Freeman.

1940   George Rieveschl, a chemical engineer in Cincinnati, Ohio, creates diphenhydramine, one of the first and most commonly used antihistamines.

1946   Diphenhydramine is approved for prescription use under the trade name Benadryl.

1966   The immunoglobulin E (IgE) antibody is discovered by Japanese scientists Kimishige and Teruko Ishizaka.

1969   T.M. Goldbert, R. Patterson, and J.J. Pruzansky publish the first large survey of cases of anaphylactic reactions to food, "Systemic Allergic Reactions to Ingested Antigens," in the journal *Allergy*.

1973   The federal Rehabilitation Act becomes law. Section 504 provides protection from discrimination for those with disabilities, including those with severe, life-threatening allergies.

1974   Swedish company Pharmacia develops the radioallergosorbent (RAST) test, used to determine what quantity of IgE antibodies (specific to suspected allergens) is present in a patient's blood.

1980s   The Food and Drug Administration (FDA) approves over-the-counter use of diphenhydramine/Benadryl.

Evolutionary biologist Margie Profet proposes the controversial theory that allergies have the protective function of driving carcinogens and other toxins from the body.

1990s   In the United States, Dr. Hugh Sampson reports that a twofold increase in allergic reactions to peanuts and other tree nuts occurred between 1985 and 1996. A doubling in the incidence of food allergies is described by doctors in England. Investigators in Germany, France, and Canada also report significant increases of various food allergies in their respective populations.

1990   The federal Americans with Disabilities Act (ADA) is passed, giving those considered to have disabilities (including those with severe allergies) the right to have their needs accommodated by public venues, including schools, child care programs, restaurants, hotels, and doctors' offices.

The Nutrition Labeling and Education Act (NLEA) becomes law, requiring that companies label foods with nutritional values such as sugar, sodium, and saturated and unsaturated fat. Although it is an important step toward protecting consumers, the act has significant exemptions that allow unlabeled allergens in food.

1992   The study "Fatal and Near-Fatal Anaphylactic Reactions to Food in Children and Adolescents," published in the *New England Journal of Medicine,* finds that of a group of children and teens who suffered fatal and near-fatal anaphylactic shock, those who survived had been administered epinephrine within five minutes of developing extreme symptoms; none of those who died were carrying epinephrine; and four of the six fatalities studied took place in school.

1996   The FDA issues an "Allergy Warning Letter" to food manufacturers urging them to clearly list any common allergens on food labels, following concerns received from consumers who had allergic reactions to unlabeled allergens in food.

A Mayo Clinic study finds that air filters on commercial airlines contain significant quantities of nut protein, suggesting the possibility of exposure to airborne allergens during flights.

2000   Farmer Delores "Dee Dee" Darden founds The National Peanut Board (NPB) to promote the interests of peanut farmers. As an important part of that effort, Darden and colleagues establish the Scientific Advisory Council (SAC), which allocates NPB funds toward researching the increase in peanut allergies.

2003   The *Mayo Clinic Proceedings* publishes a case report about a woman with a shellfish allergy who had an allergic reaction requiring hospitalization after kissing her boyfriend, who had recently eaten shrimp.

2005   The US government commits $17 million to found the National Institutes of Health (NIH) Consortium for Food Allergy Research (CoFAR), whose mission is to conduct observational and clinical studies to answer questions related to food allergies and to further understanding of the best treatment approaches.

The European Union launches the EuroPrevall Project, a multidisciplinary research project whose mission is to improve the quality of life for those with food allergies. In addition to European countries, China, India, Ghana, New Zealand, Russia, and Australia participate in the initiative.

2006   The Food Allergen Labeling and Consumer Protection Act (FALCPA) of 2004 comes into effect, requiring food labels in the United States to indicate the presence of any of the eight foods responsible for most food allergies (milk, eggs, fish, shellfish, peanuts, tree nuts, wheat, and soy), even if they are present only in trace amounts.

The NIH and Food Allergy Initiative (FAI) launch LEAP ("Learning Early About Peanut Allergy"), a large-scale study to determine whether early peanut exposure can prevent peanut allergy; the study is expected to conclude in 2014.

2008   The US National Institute of Allergy and Infectious Diseases (NIAID) launches the Exploratory Investigations in Food Allergy program, a coordinated effort to find more reliable diagnostic and treatment methods for food allergy and to investigate the origin and epidemiology of the disorder.

2009   Massachusetts passes the precedent-setting Food Allergy Awareness Act, which requires all restaurants to display a notice on menus advising patrons to alert servers to any food allergy issues; to have a certified food protection manager trained in dealing with food allergies; and to display a poster in the employee work area giving essential information on food allergies, including the major food allergens, how to accommodate food allergic patrons, signs of a reaction, and what to do in the case of a food-allergy emergency.

A study by L.H. Tonelli et al. finds increased anxiety and reduced social interaction in rodents with induced allergies.

2010   CoFAR funding is extended for another five years.

2011   A University of Dundee (Scotland) investigation discovers a defect on a gene called filaggrin that triples the risk of a child's developing a peanut allergy. The study, published in the *Journal of Allergy and Clinical Immunology*, suggests that 20 percent of those with peanut allergies carry the defective gene.

US guidelines are issued recommending food-induced anaphylaxis be treated promptly and rapidly with intramuscular epinephrine injection as a first line of treatment.

2012   A study published in the *Annals of Allergy, Asthma, and Immunology* finds a link between exposure to germicides and pesticides and the development of food allergy.

ORGANIZATIONS TO CONTACT

The editors have compiled the following list of organizations concerned with the issues debated in this book. The descriptions are derived from materials provided by the organizations. All have publications or information available for interested readers. The list was compiled on the date of publication of the present volume; the information provided here may change. Be aware that many organizations take several weeks or longer to respond to inquiries, so allow as much time as possible.

Academy of Nutrition and Dietetics
120 S. Riverside Plaza, Ste. 2000
Chicago, IL 60606-6995
toll-free: (800) 877-1600
e-mail: amacmunn@eat right.org
website: www.eatright .org

The Academy of Nutrition and Dietetics (formerly the American Dietetic Association) was founded in 1917 and is the world's largest organization of food and nutrition professionals. The academy is a multidimensional organization with seventy-four thousand members, approximately 72 percent of whom are registered dieticians. It strives to improve the nation's health and advance the profession of dietetics through research, education, and advocacy. Offerings on its website include forums, blogs, an e-newsletter, podcasts, and videos. Of particular note is the section on "Food Allergies and Intolerances."

American Academy of Allergy, Asthma & Immunology (AAAAI)
555 E. Wells St., Ste. 1100
Milwaukee, WI 53202-3823
(414) 272-6071
website: www.aaaai.org

The AAAAI is a professional organization with more than sixty-six hundred members in the United States, Canada, and seventy-two other countries dedicated to the advancement of the knowledge and practice of allergy, asthma, and immunology to improve patient care. The AAAAI publishes the *Journal of Allergy and Clinical Immunology* and the *Journal of Allergy and Clinical Immunology: In Practice*. Its website features "Ask the Expert," a searchable archive of questions and answers from health-care professionals. Of particular note on the AAAAI's website is the "Food Allergy" section, which has information on symptoms, diagnosis, treatment, and management of food allergies, and the "Just for Kids" section, which offers games, puzzles, videos, and more to help children learn about managing allergies and asthma.

The American College of Allergy, Asthma, and Immunology (ACAAI)
85 W. Algonquin Rd., Ste. 550
Arlington Heights, IL 60005
(847) 427-1200
fax: (847) 427-1294
e-mail: mail@acaai.org
website: www.acaai.org

The ACAAI, established in 1942, is a professional association of more than fifty-seven hundred allergists/immunologists and allied health professionals. Its mission is to promote excellence in the practice of the subspecialty of allergy and immunology. The organization's website has a section for patients and the public that features information on food and other allergies, online quizzes and self-tests, a search bar to find an allergist in one's local area, and tips on living with and managing allergies or asthma. The ACAAI also offers the *Patient Newsletter*, links to patient-support organizations, and stories from allergy and asthma patients. In addition, the organization maintains a presence on Twitter, YouTube, and Facebook.

American Council on Science and Health (ACSH)
1995 Broadway, 2nd Fl.
New York, NY 10023-5860
(212) 362-7044
fax: (212) 362-4919
e-mail: acsh@acsh.org
website: www.acsh.org

The ACSH provides consumers with scientific evaluations of food and the environment, pointing out both health hazards and benefits. ACSH participates in a variety of government and media events, from congressional hearings to popular magazines, and produces a wide range of publications, including peer-reviewed reports on important health and environmental topics and a semiannual review of ACSH press coverage called "Media Update." Entering "food allergies" into the ACSH website's search bar yields dozens of results, such as "Biotech vs. Peanut Allergies" and "The Anti-GM Food Circus Rolls Through Connecticut."

Anaphylaxis Canada
2005 Sheppard Ave. East, Ste. 800
Toronto, ON M2J 5B4
CANADA
toll-free: (866) 785-5660
fax: (416) 785-0458
website: www.anaphylaxis.ca

Anaphylaxis Canada was started in 2001 by a small group of people living with food and other allergies. Its mission is to inform, support, educate, and advocate for the needs of individuals and families living with the threat of anaphylaxis and to support and participate in research. Anaphylaxis Canada's website features video webinars; the *Facts + Advice Newsletter* and *Kid's Club Newsletter*; information on affiliated support groups throughout Canada; and trained staff who answer questions about allergies. Its website offers specific information for parents, educators, and health-care professionals, with sections on topics such as anaphylaxis, daily living with allergies, and allergy research.

Asthma and Allergy Foundation of America (AAFA)
8201 Corporate Dr., Ste. 1000
Landover, MD 20785
toll-free: (800) 727-8462
e-mail: info@aafa.org
website: www.aafa.org

AAFA is a not-for-profit organization founded in 1953 with the mission of improving the quality of life for people with asthma and allergic diseases through education, advocacy, and research. AAFA provides practical information, community-based services, and support to people through a network of regional chapters, support groups, and other partners around the United States. AAFA develops health education, organizes state and national advocacy efforts, and funds research to find better treatments and cures. In addition, the mission of AAFA's website is to provide online access to reliable, validated allergy and asthma information and tools to families, patients, parents, health-care providers, policy makers, and others. AAFA offers the quarterly newsletter *FreshAAIR*, the bimonthly e-newsletter *BReATHE*, and the quarterly e-newsletter *Leaders Link* (for support group leaders). Its website also offers educational programs, materials and tools, resources, the opportunity to have a professional allergist answer questions via e-mail, and information on finding a local AAFA chapter, support group, or allergy clinic.

Consortium of Food Allergy Research (CoFAR)
(301) 251-1161
e-mail: cofar@emmes.com
website: www.cofargroup.org

CoFAR was established in July 2005 by the National Institute of Allergy and Infectious Diseases (NIAID). Its mission is to conduct both observational and clinical studies to answer questions related to food allergies and to further understanding of the best possible treatment approaches. The CoFAR website's contact page has phone and address information for each of the participating centers, including the Johns Hopkins University, Mount Sinai Medical Center, and National Jewish Health. The "Food Allergy Education Program" section of the website offers a variety of information on food allergies, including how to manage food allergies inside and outside the home, avoiding allergens, and emergency treatment plans.

The Food Allergy and Anaphylaxis Network (FAAN)
11781 Lee Jackson Hwy., Ste. 160
Fairfax, VA 22033-3309
toll-free: (800) 929-4040
fax: (703) 691-2713
website: www.food allergy.org

FAAN is a nonprofit organization established in 1991 with the mission of raising public awareness, providing advocacy and education, and advancing research on behalf of all those affected by food allergies and anaphylaxis. It has a membership of approximately twenty-two thousand people worldwide, including families, dietitians, nurses, physicians, school staff, and representatives from government agencies and the food and pharmaceutical industries. FAAN staff conduct seminars and training sessions on food allergy and anaphylaxis for patients, school staff, government officials, health professionals, restaurant and food industry leaders, and other policy makers. In addition to a wealth of information on food allergies and anaphylaxis, the FAAN website offers a blog (FAANotes), e-mail alerts, videos, news releases, information on how to participate in advocacy and fund-raising, and sections for kids and teens.

Food Allergy Initiative (FAI)
515 Madison Ave., Ste. 1912
New York, NY 10022
toll-free: (855) 324-9604
e-mail: info@faiusa.org
website: www.faiusa.org

Founded in 1998 by concerned parents and grandparents, the FAI is the world's largest private source of funding for food-allergy research. FAI supports research to find a cure for food allergies; clinical programs to improve diagnosis and treatment; public policy to increase federal funding for research and to create safer environments; and educational initiatives to heighten awareness and understanding. As of 2012, FAI has committed nearly $77 million toward the fulfillment of its mission. Its website offers information on food allergies, an extensive list of support groups, an online course for educators, a resource directory, research updates, and information on clinical trials.

Food and Drug Administration (FDA)
10903 New Hampshire Ave.
Silver Spring, MD 20993-0002
toll-free: (888) 463-6332
e-mail: furls@fda.gov
website: www.fda.gov/

The FDA is a public health agency, charged with protecting American consumers by enforcing the Federal Food, Drug, and Cosmetic Act and several related public health laws. To carry out this mandate of consumer protection, the FDA has investigators and inspectors covering the country's almost ninety-five thousand FDA-regulated businesses. Its publications include government documents, reports, fact sheets, and press announcements. Entering "food allergies" into the FDA website's search bar yields thousands of results. Of particular note is the website's section on food allergens.

Kids with Food Allergies (KFA)
73 Old Dublin Pike, Ste. 10, #163
Doylestown, PA 18901
(215) 230-5394
fax: (215) 340-7674
website: http://community.kidswithfoodallergies.org

The KFA Foundation is an online educational resource whose mission is to provide families and communities with practical food-allergy management strategies in order to save lives and improve the quality of life for children and their families. It features a large online support community for families raising children with food allergies, a searchable recipe database, educational resources, a blog, videos, webinars, an e-mail newsletter, and an allergy buyer's guide that lists allergy-free and hypoallergenic foods and products. KFA also maintains a presence on Google+, Twitter, YouTube, and Facebook.

National Institute of Allergy and Infectious Diseases (NIAID)
NIAID Office of Communications and Government Relations
6610 Rockledge Dr., MSC 6612
Bethesda, MD 20892-6612
toll-free: (866) 284-4107
fax: (301) 402-3573
e-mail: ocpostoffice@niaid.nih.gov
website: www.niaid.nih.gov

NIAID is one of the National Institutes of Health. NIAID conducts and supports basic and applied research to better understand, treat, and ultimately prevent infectious, immunologic, and allergic diseases. For more than sixty years, NIAID research has led to new therapies, vaccines, diagnostic tests, and other technologies that have improved the health of millions of people in the United States and around the world. The NIAID website's section on food allergies offers food-allergy guidelines, information on research, and other information on food allergies, including sections such as "What Is an Allergic Reaction to Food?," "Eosinophilic Esophagitis and Food Allergy," and "Oral Allergy Syndrome and Exercise-Induced Food Allergy." The website also links to offerings on YouTube, Twitter, LinkedIn, flickr, and Facebook.

FOR FURTHER READING

Books

Sandra Beasley, *Don't Kill the Birthday Girl: Tales from an Allergic Life.* New York: Crown, 2011.

Robyn Brien and Rachel Kranz, *The Unhealthy Truth: How Our Food Is Making Us Sick and What We Can Do About It.* New York: Broadway, 2009.

Nicolette M. Dumke, *Allergy and Celiac Diets with Ease: Time-Saving Recipes and Solutions for Food Allergy and Gluten-Free Diets.* Louisville, CO: Adapt, 2008.

Paul J. Hannaway, *On the Nature of Food Allergy: A Complete Handbook on Food Allergy for Patients, Parents, Restaurant Personnel, Child-Care Providers, Educators, School Nurses and All Health-Care Providers.* Marblehead, MA: Lighthouse, 2007.

Janice Vickerstaff Joneja, *Dealing with Food Allergies in Babies and Children.* Boulder, CO: Bull, 2007.

Kim Koeller and Robert La France, *Let's Eat Out with Celiac/Coeliac and Food Allergies! Reference for Gluten and Allergy Free Diets.* Enhanced & rev.ed. Chicago: Gluten Free Passport, 2011.

Linda Larsen, *The Everything Food Allergy Cookbook.* Cincinnati: F+W Media, 2010.

Sloane Miller, *Allergic Girl: Adventures in Living Well with Food Allergies.* Hoboken, NJ: Wiley, 2011.

Cybele Pascal, *The Allergen-Free Baker's Handbook: How to Bake Without Gluten, Wheat, Dairy, Eggs, Soy, Peanuts, Tree Nuts, and Sesame.* Berkeley, CA: Celestial Arts, 2009.

Kelly Rudnicki, *The Food Allergy Mama's Baking Book: Great Dairy, Egg, and Nut-Free Treats for the Whole Family.* Chicago: Surrey, 2009.

Lori Sandler, *Allergy-Free Treats to Make and Share: No Nuts, Eggs, or Dairy—Just Delicious Desserts for All.* New York: St. Martin's Griffin, 2011.

PERSPECTIVES ON DISEASES AND DISORDERS

Susan Weissman, *Feeding Eden: The Trials and Triumphs of a Food Allergy Family.* New York: Sterling, 2012.

Robert A. Wood and Joe Kraynak, *Food Allergies for Dummies.* Hoboken, NJ: Wiley, 2007.

Eileen Rhude Yoder, *The Allergy-Free Cookbook: How to Avoid the Eight Major Food Allergens and Eat Happily Ever After.* Philadelphia: Running, 2009.

Judi Zucker and Shari Zucker, *The Ultimate Allergy-Free Snack Cookbook: Over 100 Kid-Friendly Recipes for the Allergic Child.* Garden City Park, NY: Square One, 2012.

Periodicals and Internet Sources

Allergy Eats! (blog), "How Much Are Food-Allergic Diners Worth?," January 4, 2011. www.allergyeats.com/blog/index.php/how-much-are-food-allergic-diners-worth.

Elizabeth Alterman, "Food Allergy Business Booms," CNBC, October 8, 2012. www.cnbc.com/id/49101728.

Melinda Beck, "Allergy-Free Dining: Restaurants Cater to Diners with Dangerous Food Issues; Flagging Plates as Safe," *Wall Street Journal,* June 14, 2012. http://online.wsj.com/article/SB10001424052702303768104577460464180837748.html.

Brooke Borel, "Can Genetically Engineered Foods Harm You?," *Huffington Post,* November 1, 2012. www.huffingtonpost.com/2012/11/01/genetically-engineered-food-health_n_2041372.html.

Jane E. Brody, "Have a Food Allergy? It's Time to Recheck," *New York Times,* January 10, 2011. www.nytimes.com/2011/01/11/health/11brody.html?_r=0 http://online.wsj.com/article/SB10001424052702303768104577460464180837748.html.

Margaret Carlson, "Deaths Show Schools Need Power of the EpiPen," Bloomberg, January 13, 2012. www.bloomberg.com/news/2012-01-13/deaths-show-schools-need-power-of-the-epipen-margaret-carlson.html.

Helen Chappell, "How a Tick Bite Made Me Allergic to Meat," *Discover,* August 31, 2012. http://discovermagazine.com/2012/jul-aug/09-how-a-tick-bite-made-me-allergic-to-meat.

Dina Colman, "Food, Unglorious Food," *Four Quadrant Living* (blog), January 17, 2012. www.fourquadrantliving.com/blog/item/64-food-unglorious-food.

Blythe Copeland, "7 Ways Food Allergies Could Actually Be Good for You—and the Earth," Treehugger, August 12, 2010. www.treehugger.com/green-food/7-ways-food-allergies-could -actually-be-good-for-you-and-the-earth.html.

Eatocracy (blog), "Peanut-Controlled Seating a Home Run for Allergy Sufferers," CNN.com, February 22, 2012. http://eatoc racy.cnn.com/2012/02/22/peanut-controlled-seating-a-home -run-for-allergy-sufferers.

Food Allergy Bitch (blog), "A Letter to the Mom Whose Son Just Died," May 17, 2012. http://foodallergybitch.blogspot .com/2012/05/letter-to-mom-whose-son-just-died.html.

Elizabeth Gordon, "Allergy-Friendly Grocery Shopping Without Breaking the Bank," *Eatocracy* (blog), CNN.com, March 29, 2012. http://eatocracy.cnn.com/2012/03/29/allergy-friendly -grocery-shopping-without-breaking-the-bank/.

Harriet Hall, "An Herbal Cure for Peanut Allergy?," Science-Based Medicine, July 29, 2008. www.sciencebasedmedicine.org /index.php/an-herbal-cure-for-peanut-allergy/#more-171.

Christopher Hassall, "A Skeptical Take on Allergy Testing," *Katatrepsis* (blog), October 10, 2012. http://katatrepsis.word press.com/2012/10/10/a-skeptical-take-on-allergy-testing.

Mark Hyman, "Are Your Food Allergies Making You Fat?," *Huffington Post*, November 3, 2009. www.huffingtonpost.com /dr-mark-hyman/are-your-food-allergies-m_b_339323.html.

Deborah Kotz, "Fighting Food Allergies: Newer Blood Tests Show That Many Children Are Misdiagnosed, While Researchers Look for a Cure," *Boston Globe*, September 3, 2012. www .bostonglobe.com/lifestyle/health-wellness/2012/09/02/when -comes-allergies-newer-blood-tests-show-that-many-children -are-misdiagnosed/Jgb5SeTqtI2JmBxnL1udAM/story.html.

Charlene Laino, "Bullied Over Food Allergies," WebMD, March 9, 2012. http://children.webmd.com/news/20120309/bullied -over-food-allergies.

Katherine Martin, "The Terror of a Food Allergy Reaction," *BabyCenter Blog*, February 2, 2012. http://blogs.babycenter .com/community_buzz/the-terror-of-a-food-allergy-reaction.

Robyn O'Brien, "The Popular Food That Turns Your Gut into a Pesticide Factory," Mercola.com, June 14, 2011. http://articles .mercola.com/sites/articles/archive/2011/06/14/why-are-there -so-many-food-allergies-now.aspx.

Anahad O'Conner, "Allergies as a Blessing in Disguise," *Well* (blog), *New York Times,* May 2, 2012. http://well.blogs.nytimes .com/2012/05/02/allergies-as-a-blessing-in-disguise.

Alice Park, "Why Black Children May Be More Likely to Develop Food Allergies," *Time,* September 5, 2011. http://healthland .time.com/2011/09/05/why-black-children-might-be-more -likely-to-develop-food-allergies.

———, "Why We're Going Nuts Over Nut Allergies," *Time,* February 26, 2009. www.time.com/time/magazine/article /0,9171,1881985,00.html.

Beth Puliti, "On Trial: Three Parents Share Their Experiences Participating in Clinical Trials," *Support Net,* Fall/Winter 2009. www.kidswithfoodallergies.org/docs/SupportNetFallWinter 2009.pdf.

Liz Rappaport, "Finding Food Allergy Allies: Schools, States, Restaurants Take Steps; Beyond the Peanut-Free Table," *Wall Street Journal,* February 28, 2012. http://online.wsj.com/article /SB10001424052970203918304577243554276460014.html.

Michael Regnier, "Food Allergy and Hyperactivity: Histories of Medical Controversy," MedicalXpress.com, September 18, 2012. http://medicalxpress.com/news/2012-09-food-allergy -hyperactivity-histories-medical.html.

Christina Tibesar, "When Food Allergies Enter the Equation," *Allergy Kids Foundation* blog, February 3, 2012. www.allergy kids.com/blog/when-food-allergies-enter-the-equatino.

UCLA Health System, "About Allergies/Future Therapies for Food Allergy." http://fooddrugallergy.ucla.edu/body.cfm?id=42.

Kathryn Vercillo, "Allergy Help: Treating Food Allergies with Chinese Medicine," Kathrynvercillo.com, October 30, 2012. http://kathrynvercillo.hubpages.com/hub/Treating-Food-Allergies -with-Chinese-Medicine.

Brian Vickery, "Could Oral Immunotherapy Be the First Treatment for Food Allergy?," Healio Pediatrics, September 1, 2010. www.healio.com/pediatrics/allergy-asthma-immunology/news /online/%7BF062C014-EC1C-4A73-8557-28D07860C250%7D /Could-oral-immunotherapy-be-the-first-treatment-for-food -allergy.

Lauren K. Wolf, "Eating Without Fear: Treatments for Food Allergies," *Chemical and Engineering News,* October 22, 2012. http://cen.acs.org/articles/90/i43/Eating-Without-Fear-Treat ments-Food.html.

INDEX

A

African American children, food allergies among, 46
Allergens, 16
  avoidance of, 23–24
Allergic Girl (Miller), 10
Allergic reactions
  cell-mediated, 27
  locations of, 20, 22
  See also Anaphylactic reaction/shock
Allergies Sourcebook, 26
American Diabetic Association (1990), 18, 25
Anaphylactic reaction/shock, 11, *21*, 22, 46
  account of parents losing child due to, 82–87
  in US, 41
  rash from, *47*
  timing of, *69*
Angioedema, *14*
Antibodies, 16
Antihistamines, 36
Atopy patch testing (APT), 30–31

B

B cells, *21*
Bachewich, Jason, 55
Benadryl (diphenhydramine), 36
Boudreau-Romano, Sarah M., 77
Branswell, Helen, 50
Bronchodilators, 36
Burks, Wesley, 40, 42, 43

C

Canadian Medical Association Journal, 51
Cancer Epidemiology, Biomarkers & Prevention (journal), *72*
Cell-mediated reactions, 27
Centers for Disease Control and Prevention
  on increase in cases of food allergy, 18
  on number of children with digestive problems/food allergies, 89
  on prevalence of food allergies in children, 40, 77
Children
  African American, allergies among, 46
  age of highest risk for fatal allergic reaction, 86
  causes of accidental food allergen ingestions in, *37*
  prevalence of food allergies among, 16, 40
Christakis, Nicholas, 12
Cross-reactivity, 22–23

D

Death(s)
  age at which children are at higher risk for, 86
  from food-related anaphylaxis in US, 22, *41*
  individuals at highest risk for, 37
Department of Agriculture, US, 23
Department of Health and Human Services, US, 52
Diphenhydramine (Benadryl), 36

E
Eczema, 56, 59, 78
Eggs, 19
Elimination diets, 34
Emergency room visits, from food-related anaphylaxis in US, *41*
Epinephrine, 24, 36–37
    percentage of administrations in school setting where allergy was unknown, 68
    in treatment of FPIES, 30
EpiPen, *86*
    number of users of, 80

F
Fish, 20
Food Allergen Labeling and Consumer Protection Act (FALCPA, 2004), 36
Food allergens, causes of accidental ingestions in small children, *37*
Food allergies
    action plans for, 38
    causes of, 18–20
    food intolerance *vs.*, 16–17
    increased awareness of, 13
    management of, 24–25, 33–38
    may be beneficial, 71–75
    personal account of mother of three children with, 77–81
    personal account of parents losing child to, 82–87
    positive effects of, *74*
    possibility of outgrowing, 38
    prevalence of, 16
    schools need to be safe for children with, 65–70
    See also Symptoms; Treatment(s)
Food Allergy and Anaphylaxis Network, 38, 68, 86

Food intolerance, 16–17
Food labels, indicating allergens, 23
Food, Nutrition & Science from the Lempert Report (website), *60*
Food protein–induced enterocolitis syndrome (FPIES), 26–32
    age distribution for onset of, *28*
Food Quality and Preference (journal), 61
Foods
    allergy-inducing, most common, 18, 19–20
    magnitude of IgG reactivity by, *58*
FPIES. *See* Food protein–induced enterocolitis syndrome

G
Gene silencing, 62
Genetic engineering, can produce less-allergenic food, 60–64
Genetically engineered crops, growth in, *63*
Glioma, 72
Gupta, Ruchi, 43

H
Hannaway, Paul J., 10
Hippocrates of Kos, 9
Hippocratic Corpus, 9
Histamine, 16, 20, 21
Hives (urticaria), 22
Hospitalizations, from food-related anaphylaxis in US, *41*

I
IBD (inflammatory bowel disease), 56
IgE. *See* Immunoglobulin E antibodies
IgG. *See* Immunoglobulin G antibody
Immune responses, type 1 *vs.* type 2, 72
Immunoglobulin E (IgE) antibodies, *21*, 27, *31*

annual testing for levels of, 38
role in allergic reactions, 20
testing for, 54, 56
Immunoglobulin G (IgG) allergy tests
are not effective, 50–54
are effective, 55–59
magnitude of reactivity, by food item, *58*
variation in, from three laboratories, *53*
Immunoglobulin G (IgG) antibody, 56
skin reaction to allergen involving, *51*
Immunotherapy, 36, 39–43
Inflammatory bowel disease (IBD), 56
Irritable bowel syndrome (IBS), 56

J
Journal of Allergy and Clinical Immunology
(journal), 43
Journal of Clinical Investigation, 73
Jung, Carl, 12

L
Lactase, 17
Lactose intolerance, 16–17
Landau, Elizabeth, 39
Lavine, Elana, 51–54
Lindberg, Kelley J.P., 88

M
Mast cells, 20, 21
Medzhitov, Ruslan, 43, 72, 73, 75
Milk, 19
Miller, Sloane, 10, 12
Moyer, Melinda Wenner, 71

N
Nadeau, Kari, 75
National Institute of Allergy and Infectious
Diseases (NIAID), 16, 20, 23
Nature (journal), 72

New England Journal of Medicine, 40, 75
Nut allergy
is life-threatening condition, 45–49
personal account of mother of child with,
88–91
Nutritional counseling, 34–35

O
Oligoantigenic elimination diets, 34
Oral allergy syndrome, 23
Oral food challenges, 38
Oral immunotherapy, 36, 38

P
Peanut allergies, 19
prevalence among children under
eighteen, *48*
Pediatrics (journal), 46
Post-traumatic stress disorder (PTSD),
11
Psoriasis, 56, 59
PTSD (post-traumatic stress disorder),
11

R
Rudnicki, Kelly, 65
Ruff, Cathy C., 33

S
Sampson, Hugh, 9
Schenk, M., 62
Schools, need to be safe for children with
food allergies, 65–70
Shellfish, 20
Shock, 29
See also Anaphylactic reaction/shock
Smulders, M., 64
Soy, 20
Stein, Joel, 46, 47

Swain, Liz, 15
Symptoms, 16, 46
    of FPIES, 29
    monitoring of, 38

T
Treatment(s), 23, 24–25
    of anaphylaxis, 36–37
    of FPIES, 29–30
    immunotherapy, 39–43
Tree nut allergies, 19
    prevalence among children under
        eighteen, *48*

U
Umetsu, Dale, 74

V
Von Mutius, Erika, 75
Vonder Meulen, Catrina, 82
Vonder Meulen, Paul, 82

W
Wall Street Journal (newspaper), 80
Wheat, 20
Wiesel, Elie, 12
Wood, Robert A., 45